DEAR SCOTLAND

DEAR SCOTLAND

On the Road with the Tartan Army

Ally McCoist

with Leo Moynihan

HODDER &
STOUGHTON

DEAR SCOTLAND

On the Road with the Tartan Army

Ally McCoist

with Leo Moynihan

HODDER &
STOUGHTON

First published in Great Britain in 2024 by Hodder & Stoughton Limited
An Hachette UK company

2

Copyright © Ally McCoist 2024

The right of Ally McCoist to be identified as the Author of the Work has been
asserted by him in accordance with the Copyright, Designs and Patents Act 1988.

A CIP catalogue record for this title is available from the British Library

Hardback ISBN 9781399739580
ebook ISBN 9781399739597

Typeset in Hewer Text UK Ltd, Edinburgh
Printed and bound in Great Britain by Clays Ltd, Elcograf S.p.A.

Hodder & Stoughton policy is to use papers that are natural, renewable
and recyclable products and made from wood grown in sustainable
forests. The logging and manufacturing processes are expected to
conform to the environmental regulations of the country of origin.

Hodder & Stoughton Limited
Carmelite House
50 Victoria Embankment
London EC4Y 0DZ

The authorised representative in the EEA is Hachette Ireland, 8
Castlecourt Centre, Castleknock Road, Castleknock, Dublin 15,
D15 XTP3, Republic of Ireland (email: info@hbgi.ie)

www.hodder.co.uk

CONTENTS

To Vivien and my boys, Alexander, Argyll, Mitchell, Arran and Harris and in memory of Walter Smith (1948 –1921)

prologue

DEAR SCOTLAND

I SHOULD start with a thank you. A thank you because these days it is with a sense of gratitude that I often find myself marvelling at my surroundings. There is no roar of the crowd, no outpouring of euphoric joy that comes with scoring a goal. Not anymore. Both were wonderful ingredients in the football career I was lucky to have, but with glory and adulation very much behind me, I can now be still. I can take in my environment and be left with a strong but quiet appreciation for the place I have always been proud to call home.

I have been fortunate enough to see much of Scotland: our coastlines, our mountains, the industrial cities, the rural towns and the fishing villages; and I am – and always will be – left with a sense of awe for the simplicity and beauty of the place where I live.

Life moves fast. An ex-footballer will always long to find a moment of contemplation, a time to close their eyes and be amongst it all again. I can close mine and be wearing the national team's iconic blue jersey. I'm one-on-one with a goalkeeper at Hampden Park; the crowd's audible expectancy is driving me forward. Their hopes are my focus, their roar is the reward for my possible success.

I can close my eyes and be with my teammates, laughing every single day. I can be with my many managers, learning from them, or maybe on the end of yet another (and perhaps deserved) rollicking. These are the memories of a career within the game I've always loved that mean more than medals and trinkets, and that is probably why I have chosen to remain in and around football.

Today my work takes me everywhere. Commentary boxes and working pitch-side will never match that feeling of being in my boots and out on that grass. But to be around the game, to hear the laughs of the players, to sense the rage and the hope of the managers, and see a ground slowly filling up in raucous expectation, is a regular reminder of what I used to do and the fun I had doing it.

I love that my work in the media takes me all over Europe and beyond, watching the best the game has to offer. I love the buzz from football's never-ending rolling news, and I love attempting to articulate the things I have learnt from the many fantastic teachers my career afforded me. Life in football is hectic, and I wouldn't change that for anything, but being able to go home, to be with my family and be still, or to get on my bicycle and visit what is around me; it never fails to soothe the soul.

My own father came from a small coastal village called Clachan, in North Kintyre on Scotland's west coast. To me, it is the most magical spot on earth. A tiny place I take my own family, and maybe it is knowing that my ancestors lived, worked and died within that beauty, that I find such solace there.

Clachan is on the magnificent cycle route known as The Five Ferries. I do it often. A route that takes you across land and sea, to and from spellbinding places with names that defy modernity. Five ferry rides from Colintraive to Rhubodach on the Isle of Bute, Rothesay to Wemyss Bay on the mainland, Ardrossan to Brodick on the Isle of Arran, Lochranza to Claonaig on the mainland and Tarbert to Portavadie; and in-between almost eighty miles of the most stunning scenery to cycle and to enjoy.

Rugged coastline, white sand beaches, wooded glens and rolling farms. A far cry from the day job. Stopping to watch for whales, or to look at the sights and be still within the beauty; as I say, the feeling I get whenever I can stop and take in Scotland is one that I only ever feel immense gratitude for.

My life as a footballer has taken me everywhere, and it started with a journey. When I signed as a keen and eager teenage footballer for St Johnstone on semi-professional forms, on St Andrew's Day (honest) in 1978, my route into work was far from straightforward.

I'd finish school at 3.45 p.m., and I would walk a quarter of a mile up to my mum's work at the United Friendly Insurance Company, where she was a secretary. I would go up the stairs, the guys would be sitting working, we'd have a wee blether, and I'd go to the kitchen where Mum always had a cup of tea and a wee roll waiting on me. I'd have that.

Then I'd leave Mum, head to the bus stop along the road, get the 4.35 bus to Buchanan Street station in Glasgow, getting off at the stop before, at Queen Street station. That would be at 5.15 and the train to Perth, the Aberdeen train, left at 5.35 p.m.

On the train there might be about ten of us, Glasgow lads playing for the club, first team and reserves. Brilliant lads. John Pelosi, Tam McNeil, big Andy Brannigan, Johnny Hamilton, loads of great guys.

We'd be on the train to Perth, I'd do my homework at the table (well, most of it), we'd arrive, get taxis to St Johnstone's stadium at Muirton, and do our training. Then we'd come back in and Mr and Mrs Gibson, a lovely couple, would have the tea made. The west-coast lads were always allowed to get the first cups and rolls. The Dundee and Perth boys would be spewing that we got preferential treatment, but that was the way it was.

We'd then get taxis back to Perth station and get the 9.45 p.m. train back down, get into Glasgow at 10.55, and the last bus would take me from Cathedral Street back up to Calderwood Square. I'd then walk the half-mile to my mum and dad's house in Ramsay Hill. Twice a week I'd do that, and loved every minute of it.

Today, I can still remember the good times, the laughs, having my shoelaces tied to the chair when I was asleep. I was sixteen years old, entering into the world of football, and to be fair, I would have travelled further just to be in the game.

Fortunately things went okay at Muirton Park. I scored some goals, and my travels getting there were just the start of a journey that led to people and to places more beautiful than I could ever have imagined. What a time it was. Magic. Games in Alloa and games in Berwick, up to Inverness and down to Queen of the South, it was always a pleasure. My rose-tinted memory bank might gloss over some of the, shall we say, adverse weather conditions, but what has stayed with me is the passion and the humour that came with plying my trade all over this country.

To play for my boyhood club, Rangers, was of course an honour and a dream come true. It came with pressures, but that's top-flight football for you. The demand is constant. Win. Simple as that. Win. As a professional you are pushed on by that weight of expectancy, and you hope to thrive on it. It becomes everything, but I also loved my time at St Johnstone, Sunderland down south, and my final spell playing at Kilmarnock, probably for different reasons to Rangers.

It was my form at the Ibrox club that allowed me to represent my country and that opportunity to play for Scotland all over the world was one that I never took for granted. Representing your country is special, and the pride taken in doing that is almost enough, but what the opportunity also brought me was the chance to meet people. By playing for my club *and* my country, I was able to work with, learn from and become friends with some of the greatest individuals the Scottish and British game has ever known.

I shared a pitch with Kenny Dalglish, I played with (and got kicked by) Graeme Souness, I grew up with Gary McAllister, scored goals with Mo Johnston, and I took passes from Paul McStay. I was rejected and then managed by Sir Alex Ferguson, I was chinned by Jock Wallace and learnt from Jock Stein, I met Sir Matt Busby, and had the absolute pleasure to do so much of it all alongside the forever wonderful Walter Smith, a man who became both a second father and the greatest of friends.

This book celebrates my experiences within the Scottish game, the stories, the glory, the pain, and the personalities who gave me so much along the way. Not all of those personalities are household names, but they are all special. There's Mr England, who took the Calderwood Stars Under-12s; Archie Robertson at my Hunter High School; Norrie Cranston at Fir Park boys club; Alex Rennie, my boss at St Johnstone; and Archie Knox, Walter Smith's longtime assistant and a man able to put me in my place if, and when, my behaviour strayed. Which, every now and then – it did.

One such occasion was with the Rangers. We were playing away at Falkirk. Walter had dropped me, and so it was with a bad attitude that I sat sulking on the bench as the action unfolded. I got on eventually, but I wasn't happy. My face was tripping me, as we say up here. My mood was further affected when I was well in on goal, but our winger, Dale Gordon, didn't square the ball to me.

We won the game, but back in the dressing room, I was spewing. I'd been dropped, I'd not scored, my teammate hadn't passed to me, and things in my world were as bad as they could be. Or that is how I saw it anyway, and like a teenager without their phone, I was going to let everyone know about it. Basically, I was going to act like an idiot. A real idiot.

Archie was going about the dressing room. 'Those of you who played today, you're off tomorrow,' he said. My ears pricked up. 'Those of you who never played, and those who got on as subs, you're in tomorra mornin'.' My mood blackened. I looked up at him.

'I'll no be fuckin' in, in the mornin',' I say.

Archie gives me a look that suggests he's heard me, but must have misheard me, and he repeats the statement.

'Boys who played today, you're off tomorra, Lads that never played and the subs, see you in the mornin'.'

'I'll no be in on the morra.' I've now gone fully rogue and Archie is having none of it.

'Oh, you'll be fuckin' in on the morra,' he says.

'I tell you what, I'll no be in on the morra.' At this point my behaviour gets even worse as I jut out my chin and say, 'And there it is if you fancy a slice of it.'

Well, Archie has flown at me. Quite right too. It's gone off in this tight wee dressing room at the old Brockville Park. It's mayhem, we're being thrown off each other and Archie is spewing at my juvenile behaviour. I know I am wrong but there is no going back, and in the middle of us both is a team that have just won away from home and should be quietly celebrating the fact.

Not me, I'm not celebrating and eventually, with the bedlam controlled, my teammates have their say. 'You're a fuckin' idiot, you,' is a common response. They are right, of course, but I take my sulk and I go and shower alone. In strolls Walter. He'd been with the press during the mayhem, but word has got back to him, and he wants to have his say.

'Oh you!' he says, hands in his pockets. He's not happy.

'Wha' is it?'

'Wha' is the matter with you?'

'Nothin'.'

'Wha' is the matter with you?'

'Oh, you no playing me, and him no passing to me, and Archie making me come training . . .'

'It's no about you! We've won away from home, stop being an idiot. Now you get outta here and go apologise to Archie.'

'I will, I'm sorry,' I say, Walter's stern wisdom, as ever, waking me up to my own shoddy behaviour.

Walter goes to turn away, then he comes back and says, 'And another thing, you do know, don't you?'

'Know wha'?'

'That you're in tomorra.'

I got showered and dressed and before we left, I held my hands up to my unacceptable behaviour, and took some stick from the lads. Archie put it behind us and the next day I came into Ibrox for training. I walked to the home-team dressing room and up above the door, Archie and Walter had fashioned a huge banner and upon it were the words: 'RANGERS FOOTBALL CLUB WOULD LIKE TO TAKE THIS OPPORTUNITY TO WELCOME ALLY McCOIST TO TRAINING THIS MORNING!'

I fell about laughing at the sheer genius of it, and it was the perfect example of how people like Archie and Walter made my life in football such a pleasure, even when I was not at my best. I must have driven them insane at times, but my word, we had a laugh along the way, and it was anecdotes such as that, and the great people like Walter and Archie, that gave me as much pleasure as the goals, the trophies and the caps.

As did the Scottish public. The Tartan Army have filled stadiums to watch Scotland, from Hampden in the Mount

Florida area of Glasgow to the Rocky Mountains in Denver, Colorado, and to have been given the opportunity to play in front of them meant everything. Today, as a pundit and co-commentator travelling to watch Scotland, I am left only with pride at the fun, colour, humour and passion that the Tartan Army takes with them, wherever they go.

It was Winston Churchill who once said that when it comes to small countries and the contribution they have made to mankind, Scotland can only be matched by the ancient Greeks. I'm not sure about all that, but as an ancient foot-baller who once scored against Greece, who am I to argue. For me, one of those great contributions, maybe even up there with the telephones and the televisions we gave the planet, is the wonderful support that follows our national football team.

Of course, those hearty and merry souls are often left disappointed. Having stood amongst them, and watched far-flung tournaments as a youngster on the TV, then gone on to play in three major competitions myself, I share the pain and the frustration that so often goes with that incredible support.

In Scotland, though, we persevere, and I suspect that the same optimism, hope and (often blind) belief will continue to follow the football team for generations to come. Perseverance, optimism and humour come with being Scottish. There are times, be it watching the football, or step-ping out on a winter's morning, that we require all three collectively, but I am firmly of the belief that the people we live amongst and the beauty that surrounds us more than make up for any hardships.

Football has been my life, it has taken me to all four corners of the world, and today I still love to pack a bag and go to watch a match. Wherever that may be. The thing is, and this will never change, the greatest part of any trip away is coming home.

Dear Scotland . . . I thank you.

one

LET THERE BE ROCK

I AM standing on a football pitch. I'm right where I want to be. Where I've always wanted to be. The faultless turf shimmers under my feet, it feels wonderfully familiar. The floodlights above burn their glare down upon us, illuminating the night, making the occasion and the moment even more exhilarating.

Then there's the noise. That sound that does something to a footballer's reactions, which quickens the heart and focuses the mind. The noise of a crowd's roar welling up, becoming more guttural, and with each octave it's as if needles are piercing the skin, injecting all their devotion and passion into a footballer's bloodstream until he'll run through a wall for them.

I'm standing on a football pitch, and as that sound rises into the German night, for one fleeting second I am a footballer again. For one brief moment, it brings all those feelings surging back. But then reality strikes, the players are running onto the pitch to start their extensive warm-ups, and the roar is for them, no one else, and rightly so; the gladiatorial stars of every major international tournament.

Those heady, joyous days are over. Today I am part of a television team. Don't get me wrong, I adore it. There is nothing like playing, there will never be anything like it, but when time makes its inevitable move on us, covering these competitions for television and radio, being around the most dedicated, fun-loving and talented bunch of colleagues – well, it's as close as you can get without putting your shin-pads on.

That night on 14 June 2024, I am standing with the great Laura Woods. We are doing pieces to camera from the pitch. It is Munich. The opening game of the European Championships, at the remarkable Allianz Arena. The hosts are playing and their players glide onto the pitch, that noise lifting them, reminding them of the support they'll have everywhere they go, but also the expectation a nation will place on their shoulders. Their opponents are Scotland. My lot. The Scots players sprint onto the field, each step made in defiance of form and logic.

Laura and I are doing our work, when that roar rises up. The home fans, brutally confident, ready to cheer their team all the way to the final. The Scots, the Tartan Army, somehow even louder, their screams fuelled by unabashed patriotism, unparalleled hope and enough local beer to fill Loch Ness. The mood is electric. Everything is ahead of us. For an international footballer, there can be no better feeling than the start of a tournament. As I say my words to Laura, to the camera and the audience back home, my mind drifts back to my playing days.

Being away, representing Scotland, my country, a place I have loved since forever. Being with my teammates, allowing ourselves to believe that this time will be our time. Training, laughing, so much laughing, playing in front of and for our Scottish supporters, many of whom have spent money they don't have to be there, but who consistently show the world the very best of our nation. Time has changed most things, my legs certainly won't do what my heart desires, but as I look out at a mass of fellow Scots, I realise that time cannot hinder their passion or their support. I miss it. Time to stop reminiscing now. There's work to be done.

I arrived in Munich two days ago. For what seemed months, my media work on television and radio has been leading up to this. Everything has been gearing up to a competition that promises so much for so many British fans.

The English fans are hoping, no, demanding that this year, with this set of talented individuals, they can at last add to that World Cup of 1966. For Scots (in addition to hoping that they do not), there is the promise of history. The team's form in the qualifying rounds has been special, the likes of Spain have been beaten, and with results like that, the country has understandably allowed itself to fall into a collective sense of hope. We've been there before, and we will be there again.

Since I fell in love with the game in the late 1960s, Scotland have been sending their best footballers onto planes and onto coaches, away to take on the world. They have been putting them into fitted suits, the people have lined the streets, and they have waved them off to faraway foreign lands.

Many from our nation have followed them across oceans, continents and hemispheres. Walking, flying, driving, by trains and boats – on one occasion it is said even a submarine was used, and having met a fair few of these brave and intrepid souls, I have no reason to disbelieve it.

And so to Germany for another crack at footballing immortality. For the players chosen this time there is no delusion of winning it, but at least a hope to prosper, to win a football match or two, to reach the knockout stages, where no Scottish squad has ventured before, which would bring each of them heroic status usually reserved for those with militaristic motives who have seen their English equivalents away down the road.

Arriving in Munich, a place I have been to several times before, brought the occasion to life. I won't say that the time for talking was over (as a broadcaster that might prove problematic), but to be in a city with such a rich footballing heritage, the drive from airport to hotel brought those pre-tournament tingles flooding back.

You can feel it in the air. The drivers are talking about it, the bars with their flags and extra kegs are prepared for it, the hotel staff enthusiastically ask your opinion on it. A nation is ready. A continent is ready. I'm ready, but first, I want to reintroduce myself to an old friend . . .

I have loved AC/DC for a very long time. My pals and I used to go to gigs in Glasgow as youngsters. By now, plenty of people know the love I have for the band, thanks mainly to a clip of me on duty with TNT Sports, prior to a Champions League quarter-final at the Allianz Arena in Munich in April 2024. Preparing to go on air, a song started on the Tannoy. The bells immediately caught my attention. 'That cannae be AC/DC.' It was, and the images of my well-practised but limited air-guitar seemed to make people laugh, and to the surprise and pride of my kids (they care little for the various European Golden Boots I won as a player), I went viral.

It was 'Hells Bells' by AC/DC and I am right on that short clip when I say, 'You cannae beat a bit of AC/DC, man.' You can't! It was early November 1980 when we all made it to the Glasgow Apollo to see them on their *Back in Black* tour, and to a man we were blown away. I still am. 'Hells Bells' was the opening tune that night, and so when I hear that intro, those bells and then that guitar, wherever I may be, you will get a reaction. It may be gentle air-guitar or it may be a full-on head-bang, but you will get a reaction. Absolutely magic.

Talking of reactions, that viral clip seemed to get many people's attention, including the Scottish comedian, Grado. Grado is a very funny guy, and soon after my clip's newfound fame, he made his own, sending me up, but changed the music to Whigfield's 'Saturday Night'. I was in hysterics when I saw it. 'You cannae beat a bit of Whigfield, man!' Well, I was in hysterics for the first 312 times I saw it. After that, when every person on the planet I knew, and quite a few of the people I didn't know, had sent me the same clip, the novelty wore off a wee bit.

I did call Grado though. He must have seen my name come up on his phone and wondered if I was calling for a rant. As well as his comedy, Grado is also a wrestler, so even if I had taken offence, I think he knew he was getting away with it. We had a right good giggle about it.

'Clatty Pats, 1994!' was the venue he chose in his clip. That had me rolling on the floor. Clatty Pats for the poor souls who don't know is what people called Cleopatra's nightclub off the Great Western Road, in the West End of Glasgow. A lively old place, to say the least.

My first night in Munich and it is not nightclubs I'm looking to get into, it is the Olympic Stadium, Bayern Munich's old stadium. AC/DC are doing a gig there and there is no way I am going to miss out. Mind you, the omens are not good. On both occasions I came to the stadium with Rangers to play Bayern, I was injured and didn't play. I am fighting fit now though and pull a few strings to get inside.

I have a good friend, Robbie, a great lad from Glasgow, and it's Robbie who gets me the tickets for the gig. Robbie used to be AC/DC's tour manager, which is very handy, and he puts in a few calls and we have our tickets. What a magical night. Because the band have been on the go for so long, the difference in ages of the fans at their gigs is incredible. People in their seventies, with their kids and their grandkids.

What a mix there is in that famous old stadium, and what a show the band put on. Malcolm and Angus Young were both born in Glasgow, and spent their early years in the city. Malcolm has sadly passed on now, but years ago, my mate Robbie brought Malcolm and Malcolm's son up to a game at Ibrox, and we have some fantastic photos of myself and them holding up Rangers jerseys, one with Malcolm on it, and one with Angus on it. Great lads. Great memories.

I quickly have the idea to do another video, me at the gig, hearing the start of 'Hells Bells' again. 'Is this AC/DC?' This time with the band 100 metres away from me. We manage to get it right and end up howling with laughter. I'll say it again, 'You cannae beat a bit of AC/DC!'

Standing in that stadium, there are three lads right in front of us. I am enjoying the concert, rocking out, and these lads are enjoying a few beers, when one turns around to me and says, 'We don't want to bother you during the gig, Ally, but us three are from Bishopton,' which is effectively the next village along from mine. Unbelievable. We have a right good laugh. A few of us lads from the small villages nestled on the west coast of Scotland and we're having it large at an AC/DC gig in Bavaria. What a beautiful but small world.

Actually, it is no surprise to find myself next to three Bishopton boys, because by the time I arrive in the city of Munich, the place is awash with tartan. By the tens of thousands, Scots have descended on the place. Everywhere you look, there are red-cheeked, smiling faces. The beer halls are rocking to the boisterous thunder of the Tartan Army's substantial playlist. 'I'm Gonna Be (500 Miles)', 'We'll Be Coming', 'Yes, Sir, I Can Boogie', 'No Scotland, No Party' and, of course, 'Flower of Scotland'; they all boom into the night sky. They even give AC/DC a run for their money on the sound stakes.

It is home from home, and on the second night, the eve of the opening game, I am on my way to co-host a charity function that will raise loads of money for many good causes, including Street Soccer, the homeless football charity back home. Nearly £600,000 is raised, which is incredible, and whilst doing so we all have the best night.

It is a bit of a who's who of Scottishness. Big names in business such as Sir Tom Hunter and Lord William Haughey. People willing to put their hands in their pockets. The actor, Martin Compston, who was a very good footballer, and Gordon Smart, the broadcaster. Plenty of old teammates are there too. Gary McAllister, Darren Fletcher, The Big Eck Alex McLeish, James McFadden, Neil McCann and big Stevie Thompson, amongst others.

I am doing a five-minute chat on the stage with Sir Alex Ferguson and my first question to him takes him back to the days when I was a young footballer, and he would pick me up at the house after school. Myself and another lad, Stevie Cowan. Sir Alex used to stay in East Kilbride and would take us over to Paisley to train with the kids at St Mirren, whilst he took the first team. We would then wait, nipping round to get a bag of chips, before Sir Alex would drive us back home. We go a long way back.

So I am reminding him of those old days, thanking him for the lift. The thing is that when push came to shove, he didn't sign me as a kid, choosing Stevie Cowan instead. 'Sir Alex,' I say, reminding him of those heady days. 'One of your first jobs was at St Mirren, and it was there that you failed to sign the double European Golden Boot winner, Ally McCoist. That would have finished off most young coaches and managers, but to be fair to you, you made a half-decent comeback.'

Sir Alex howls with laughter, before grabbing the microphone and telling the audience a few home truths about me and putting me firmly back in my place.

The best line of the night goes to my co-host, the comedian Fred MacAulay. Fred is a ridiculously funny man, and we have four musicians up on stage with us. Dougie Vipond from Deacon Blue, the brilliant Amy Macdonald, Johnny Mac from the Bay City Rollers, and Dougie Payne, the bass player from Travis, who is a lovely lad.

Fred is interviewing him, and they are talking about what Travis has been up to, and he says they have just come off a tour supporting The Killers. He tells us that The Killers were brilliant to work with, that the lead singer Brandon Flowers is a diamond, and that they would love to work with them again.

Fred turns around, looks at the wee guy from Bay City Rollers, and says, 'He's worked with the Killers too – unfortunately it was Rose and Fred West.' Totally from leftfield, the place falls about laughing and I almost fall off the stage.

The night is a major success, the bands and the singers all play, that big total is raised for charity, and to show my professionalism – knowing that I am on television doing the Scotland game the following night and wanting to look after my precious voice – I head home early to my bed.

The last thing I see, as I am leaving, is Fred MacAulay grabbing the microphone from the Travis frontman, Fran Healy, convinced that he could belt out a better chorus of 'Why Does It Always Rain On Me' than Fran himself. Time to go, Ally. Time to go.

As I sit in my room, I'm thinking about the chat I have just had on stage with the former Scotland players about what it is like on the eve of a tournament. Each of us recalls that sense of anticipation we felt, the excitement, and of course sometimes the dread! Like the punters who travel to see us, every emotion runs through you. The night before a game, the players in the hotel will be feeling the same, hopefully without the dread, but they will be knowing that they are less than a day away from folklore or ridicule. It's an odd place to be. I turn the light off, and unlike the boys in the squad, I fall into a deep sleep.

The following morning. The day of the match and you can feel the excitement in the air. The hosts are amazing. The Germans know how to put on an event like this. Football is everything here. You sense it everywhere you go. The success they have had over the years, the players they have produced, the mark the country has left on the game, be it manufacturers such as Adidas and Puma, or historic tournaments of yesteryear, you cannot deny the Germans their place firmly at football's top table.

Whilst they are excited for their team's chances – and as hosts housing some fine young players they must be amongst the favourites – the people of Munich are fascinated with the 100,000-plus visitors who have not stopped singing and drinking (two of Bavaria's most popular pastimes) for days. The Germans and the Scots have a lot in common. Okay, one has a few more of those wee stars on their football shirts, we won't delve into that, but the people are very much alike.

They love their football and they love a drink, not to get violent, but to be merry, have a singsong and get on with it. The Scots have this way of drinking and then loving you to death. It's a skill and the locals can't get enough. Eventually it is hard to make out where the kilts start and the lederhosen stop. Both kind of blend into one.

The night of the game and the spirits are high. Very high. In fact, news goes around that the beer halls of Munich have run out of stock and orders are being made up from elsewhere. It takes some sort of session to drink Munich dry, I can tell you that. How have the Germans allowed it to happen? I'm not sure if it says a lot for my country and our people's capacity to sink an ale or two, or it totally bursts the myth that the Germans are the most efficient race on the planet.

Having said that, walking into the Allianz, the most aesthetically pleasing stadium around, and all those thoughts of efficiency rush back. It is a fantastic arena, and as we get to work, and with both teams now kitted out and ready for the anthems, the heart is racing and the adrenaline is pumping faster than a Munich beer tap.

We've been there for four hours now, doing all sorts of pieces. The stuff on the pitch with Laura, with that special noise making it impossible to hear each other and, to be honest, at times I am guessing what she's saying. I also do a bit with the Scottish Television guys, so I am up and down from pitch to gantry, but then we settle in to the commentary position, where I like to go over my notes and prepare for the kick-off.

Then there's the anthems. The German one is rousing enough, but I have never heard 'The Flower of Scotland' sung with such gusto at a football match. I have always heard it best at Murrayfield, prior to the rugby, but stood here, in Munich, looking to my left and seeing the thousands who have got in, it is magical, knowing there are even more in the bars and fan parks nearby, let alone those still at home. One of the very best. Right up there with Murrayfield, if not even better, and I do not say that lightly.

If the raised and passionate voices of over 20,000 hopeful Scots can lift the spirits, then it takes only the sound of a referee's opening whistle to stifle them. From the very off, the team look overawed; from the first second, it is obvious there is a problem. I hate to use the term 'froze' because I know, as much as anyone, how hard tournament football can be, let alone when you face the Germans, the hosts, but it is abundantly clear from the start that the occasion has got to them. Before they get their bearings, we are three-nothing down, a player has been sent off, and it's halftime. Welcome to the Euros, lads.

The whistle for the interval goes, there's a pause, then Sam Matterface, the commentator, says his piece, we go to the adverts, Sam takes off his ear-piece and I take mine off. There is another pause and we just look at each other, open-mouthed. *That didn't go according to plan.*

The second half is a tiny bit better. It's hard to work out if the Germans have simply taken their foot off the gas, or Scotland have got a little more organised. Our fans don't stop singing, and whilst a few must have been gasping for a pint, there are no empty spaces. Their devotion is rewarded with an albeit scrappy goal, but the killer blow in the last minute is the fifth goal. It sounds silly, but that is the one that hurts the most.

We might have drawn the second half: 4–1. Okay, not good but let's get up the way, out of here and back to the hotels. And then they score. It's five. Five. Four is a beating, but five, that's a battering. It's a psychological thing but it's true. Five. Oh bollocks. We've been battered.

Our work is done, and we skulk back to the hotel, where a few beers are a necessity after a night like we've had. They are going down well when a group of Germans approach us, big smiles on their faces, understandably so. There is a bit of patter flying about, and I sense a slight delight in my own deflation. Okay, okay, that's fine. I get it. We get up to leave, and we're shaking hands. I grip one guy with a firm shake, he wishes us all the best and I say, 'The only good news we can take from tonight is that we won't see you again until the final.'

With that, and with the Germans staring at me like I have lost my marbles, I stroll off to my bed. Tomorrow, after all, is another day . . .

two

ON THE MARCH

SCOTLAND is the only nation on the planet with rain that's sole purpose is to cause bodily harm. Scottish rain is not like other rain. I've been places. Florida, Asia, yes, they have torrential downpours, but the raindrops in these far-off lands are big, warm globules. Not at home. In Scotland the rain is *sore* rain. It drives in at a 65-degree angle, and seems to consist of tiny shards of glass designed, as far as I can tell, to draw blood.

It was into this sore rain, on a supposedly early summer's day in 1978, that my dad and my fifteen-year-old self took ourselves out for a trip to Hampden Park, to see off a football team that some had started to believe could soon be crowned champions of the world. Scotland, with a plethora of footballers shining bright in the domestic, English and European game and led by their mad scientist of a manager, Ally MacLeod, who had made claims about how far they could go in the tournament to be held in Argentina.

Comments on the record about bringing home a medal had grown men starting to wonder – hard-working men not usually susceptible to hyperbole – and when MacLeod himself uttered the word *winners*, dreams began to form in even the most stoic of Scottish hearts.

The thing about such grandiose comments is that they poked at one of the most vulnerable and perhaps most endearing traits of us Scottish folk. Optimism. We all have it. Don't be fooled by the dour exterior that some of my countrymen give off. That's for show. It is for classic sitcoms like *Porridge* with the brilliantly and consistently upset Mr Mackay, or *Dad's Army* and Private Frazer, whose famous line 'We're doomed!' might have been said by any of us with a mere glance at the weather forecast.

The truth is, that stereotype is only half right. Scots are in fact the most optimistic people on earth, it's just that we also like to act dour. It's a brilliant paradox that we have given the world. We've always had to have a bit of both. Dourness comes from knowing something bad is around the corner, the optimism comes from centuries of dealing with whatever it might be.

Look at our ancestors. For eons they have faced the threat of invasion. From Vikings crossing the North Sea to the English coming from the south. We have had it from all angles. Over time it has built up a resilience in our DNA. Whilst the threat of pillaging Scandinavians no longer exists and the English seem to have got bored of marauding our lands, we remain a resilient people. There's always a sense that things are going to be okay.

Listen to 'Auld Lang Syne', a Scottish song now sung around the world on New Year's Eve. Things are going to be okay. Tomorrow will be better.

If those invasions have stopped, the weather continues to attack us. When discussing the wind up here, the great Billy Connolly wasn't joking when he said most of Shetland's trees are in Norway. It's just part of life up here. Everyone knows that you're better off wearing a crash helmet rather than using an umbrella, and a suit of armour would be preferable than a raincoat, but no matter, out we went on that day in 1978, with the rain cutting into us but failing to ruin the occasion.

My dad and I had left East Kilbride, our new town, for Hampden Park, the famous old stadium, and we pitched up in a pub nearby with his pals and their kids. Us youngsters were, of course, left outside the establishment. People of a certain age will know that kids in the 1970s and 1980s were often asked to entertain themselves outside public houses, munching on what seemed like 2,472 packets of crisps.

They were magic times, being around the adults, hearing the odd swear word (actually a lot of swear words) and being part of the occasion. On this particular day, the occasion was seeing off the Scotland squad, who had chosen to have an open-top bus parade prior to leaving for the World Cup. To my young self, the decision seemed to be both optimistic and beautifully realistic. We all want to celebrate the team, we all want to have a party, but it's probably best to do a leaving one rather than rely on a heroic return.

And so on we went towards Hampden. Glasgow's streets were full of optimistic smiles. The dads – the pints of Heavy fuelling their stride – walked ahead, whilst us younger lads, undeterred by that ton of crisps, smiled and sang along with the crowd. 'We're on the march with Ally's army!' was on everyone's lips. Sung by Andy Cameron and written by Samuel Dennison, the official Scotland World Cup song 'Ally's Tartan Army' was a huge hit that summer, and as the stadium grew closer, it was all you could hear.

Andy's song had become a summer anthem. Later I became great friends with him, and he had me in stitches when he told me about the time he performed his hit on the TV show *Top of the Pops*. Andy had travelled down to London for the show with his dad. With him in the green room was Billy Idol, performing with Generation X. Billy must have taken offence at wee Andy with his football kit on and tartan tam o' shanter hat, because he turned to him and said, 'Who the fuck are you?'

Well, Andy wasn't having that. He flew at him and soon everyone was trying to pull them apart. Andy's dad jumped in, Billy's band were involved. There was tartan everywhere. It was all going off. Now, if I had been there, I would have jumped in for my fellow countryman too, but if I am honest, by then my musical tastes were already leaning towards the punks he was fighting.

The late 1970s were a magic time to be a teenager in Scotland. The optimism and hope felt so keenly that day at Hampden was nothing new to me and at fifteen, me and my gang were obsessed with music. Big Stevie Kerr, Midge, Sammy, Wee Davey, Alan, Hefty, Housty, Knoxy, Big Jock, Wee Bic, and myself. We were a tight crew. Loved our football, loved our music, and that music was mainly punk.

Loads of the guys did the full bit. Mohicans, dyed white-blond hair, skinheads, bovver boots, chains; all of that. I have to admit that I was saved by my football from going all-out punk. Well, football and the fact that my mum and dad would have given me a clip around the ear if I had.

I loved the punk scene, and would wear some of the clothes and the boots, but I was grateful to have an excuse not to go all the way with the mad hair and all of that. 'Sorry, lads,' I'd say. 'Got a match this Saturday, you'll have t'get the chain piercings without me.'

We'd do everything together, and are still in touch today. We have a WhatsApp group, and the jokes still flow like the old days. But now, instead of being punks, we organise golf days. We've gone from wanting to smash up the world with our youthful rage, to wondering whether to take a nine iron or a sand wedge at the 16th hole.

Back then, we were full of it. We would meet most Friday nights, have a few tins of lager at the Smokies, a patch of grass near the bus stop in Calderwood, and then on to the 77 or 79 bus into Glasgow and the Apollo. What a venue. There we'd see The Clash, The Undertones, The Jam, Devo, Killing Joke, Sham 69, and many others.

One night we went to see Sham 69 and during the gig, our pal, wee Sammy, went missing (his real name was Alan McIlroy, so we named him Sammy after the Manchester United player Sammy McIlroy – football was never far from our thoughts).

'Where's Sammy?'

'Fuck knows.'

'How's he missin' this gig, man?'

All of a sudden, wee Sammy walked onto the stage. He was up there with Sham 69. A teenager from Calderwood, and he was up on stage, arm in arm with the lead singer, Jimmy

Pursey, and together they were belting out 'If the Kids are United'. Oh. My. God. Away they went, the crowd were going wild and our lot were screaming our approval. What a moment. Sammy took the applause and walked off.

What we didn't know there in the mosh pit was that the venue's bouncers were not giving Sammy such a welcome reception. He got into a fight with a couple of the bouncers, and after the gig, with no sign of our pal, we headed out towards the Blue Lagoon, a local chippy.

In there, we found Sammy. He looked a right sight. His nose was at 45 degrees, blood was trickling from his eye, his lip was split, and he was ordering a couple of pickles to go with his fish supper. He turned to us and without flinching, he said, 'Before you ask, it was well worth it.'

We couldn't stop laughing, and that's pretty much how we lived our teenage years. Listening to music, going to football and laughing. As I say, we'd sneak in a few tins of lager, but there was never any sign of any drugs back then. Those problems were soon to come to Scotland but the whole *Trainspotting* thing wasn't in our lives. A few of the lads would try a cigarette, a great guy called Davie Mackie (or Wee Bic as we called him) even carried around a pipe. A teenage boy with a pipe in the back pocket of his jeans? That didn't last long, I can tell you. We're all getting on now, though, so maybe it's time to all have one.

As teenagers we'd do the Boys' Brigade (4th East Kilbride) together, and go on holidays with the BB to far-flung places like the Isle of Wight and Guernsey without our parents. They were magic lads, and we were having the time of our lives.

It was a tragedy that brought us back together. Big Stevie,

an integral part of the group, passed away a few years back, and as tragic as his death was, it led to us all getting back into contact. Stevie was a big, lovable guy and one of the greatest gifts he left was bringing the gang back together. The big man would like that.

The great thing about that time was this unerring sense that anything was possible. We were punks, and whilst in reality we had nothing but respect for our parents and elders, there were establishments to topple. From 1976, when the Sex Pistols suddenly appeared on the ITV show *Today* with Bill Grundy in England, a bunch of teenagers with their feet on the table and swearing live on television, things changed. Their album *Never Mind the Bollocks*, with its songs about anarchy, became a soundtrack to our lives.

The day after the group's television outbursts, the *Daily Mirror* ran a headline: 'THE FILTH AND THE FURY!' they cried. I'm not sure about filth, but the fury raged through the music, and I think a lot of that energy was in Scottish hearts at that time too.

And so it was with the football team. Take that famous, or infamous, day at Wembley Stadium in 1977. Gordon McQueen's towering header, Kenny Dalglish's goal, which turned out to be the winner. I became great pals with Gordon as we lived in the same village. The nicest of guys, so funny, the big man could kill you with a one-liner. Sometimes I'd sit there in the golf club laughing my head off with him, and I'd think, I was watching you on my telly tower above the England defence before slamming a header past Ray Clemence to open the scoring and send Scotland's hordes of supporters into raptures.

Those fans, of course, would mark the day with perhaps overly zealous celebrations – the goals became climbing frames before collapsing and the pitch was slightly ploughed – but there was no malice. To this day, guys from Inverness, Bishopbriggs, Grangemouth and beyond continue to claim that a piece of Wembley still grows there in their back gardens. Who knows if they are telling the truth but I, for one, hope they are.

That day remains lodged in Scottish folklore. The crowd must have been over 600,000 because most of Scotland says they were there. I was not. My first Wembley trip would come two years later, but as a teenager, I do remember feeling that if our national team could topple England in their Empire stadium, why couldn't we take on and beat the world's footballing establishments? As Vivienne Westwood incorporated tartan in her punk designs, why couldn't our country be the punks of world football?

My own establishment, my mum and dad, had given me a love of football. Both Neil and Jessie McCoist were keen fans of the game, and I cannot remember a time when the feats of players from home, England and abroad were not a topic of conversation in our home.

My father's home had been Clachan, a small but beautiful village in North Kintyre, on Scotland's west coast. With about fifteen houses, it's a world away from Glasgow's football scene, but I continue to visit what I consider one of the most beautiful places on earth. I never knew my paternal grandpa, but he was the gatekeeper at a hunting and fishing lodge, and must be the reason for my love of both. My mum never liked me hunting, so I'd have to tell her that it was in my blood. I also love to walk and cycle and I visit Clachan to do both at least three times a year.

Now that my dad has passed, the place is the only real link to our family name's past. I'm pretty sure there are no other McCoists in the United Kingdom (if there are any, please get in touch). There are some relatives in Australia but it is Clachan, in its gorgeous wee church, that the family name remains. In the graveyard, there are some gravestones with the family, sometimes spelt with a K, and on the church wall, a commemorative plaque celebrates the names of those villagers who went to war, including that of my grandfather.

My sons didn't meet their grandad – my dad died when my first wife was four months pregnant with our first – but they love to make the trip to Clachan. I love those visits. I love that my lot enjoy them so much too, and how much the family feel at home there. The people there are all so friendly. I am not sure if they know me as a footballer (and why should they?), and we always feel very welcome.

My mum, Jessie, was from Glasgow, one of five kids, daughter to the amazing wee Jeanie Agnew, the most brilliant woman you ever met, and my mum was very similar. My grandfather had died suddenly and Jeanie was left to bring up their five kids. Auntie Irene, Auntie Beth, Auntie Chris, my mum and big Uncle George.

My mum would tell me about when she was very young, of how their community rallied around Jeanie after my grandfather died. She'd tell me about people bringing food, and offering any money they had spare. These were not well-off people, you understand, but that sense of community always stayed with me. It was old school, and meant that my young mum and her siblings were able to grow up feeling loved and secure. My wee granny, Jeanie, made sure of that and worked tirelessly.

More of Jeanie later, but with my grandfather's passing, it meant that my Uncle George was man of the Agnew house, and it seemed to be the making of him. George was a big, hard man, but he was lovable and kind. In some ways, he later became the family protector, but in honesty without George, the family, my immediate family, might not have existed.

But for George and football, my mum and dad would not have met. You could say I exist thanks to football. My dad had moved to Glasgow to work as a fitter at Weir Pumps, an engineering company, and there he met George playing in the firm's football team, before joining him to play weekend games with the Methodist church.

I can tell you, those church games were not for Sunday School kids. These were tough games, played by hard men. If you came off with a pulse you were ecstatic. George and my dad got on famously, and it wasn't long before he introduced his teammate to his family, including his sister, Jessie, and that was that. Jessie Agnew became Jessie McCoist.

Glasgow was changing and post-war towns had sprung up to house new residents. Mum and Dad looked to East Kilbride, the first of these new towns, as the place to settle. My mum loved to tell the story of how she went along for an interview regarding a council house. Mum was pregnant with my older sister, Alison. Lots of people were looking to make similar moves from Glasgow, but in this meeting, the lady took one look at her, and said, 'I didn't realise you were pregnant.' After that, the interview was a very short one. Not long after, my parents got the news. They had got the council house, but not only that, they had got one at the end of a terrace, with a wee bit of a garden.

My mum was certain that the woman who interviewed her had given us the house with the garden because she wanted us kids to have a bit of space. My mum never forgot the lady's kindness, and by the way, without that act of kindness, I may never have become a footballer, because to me growing up, that wee space, something like four metres by four metres, became Hampden Park for me and my young pals.

Football had become everything to me. My family had made sure of that, and as my wee mum loved having people around, the local kids would come to mine for a game of two-a-side. Without knowing it, with just big smiles on our faces, we began to understand how the football bounced, how to get it under our control, and generally how to play. Playing other games such as 'Kerbie' on the pavement were also pivotal to so many youngsters learning about and gaining football skills.

If the games got bigger and more serious, which they did, a load of us would head up to The Hill, a bit of grass big enough for us all. The routine was the same. School finishes, run home, throw your bag in by quarter to four, go out and start the match, get a shout for your dinner at half five, consume that in record time (my personal best was three minutes), back out at quarter to six, and play on until dark. In the summer that might be 10 o'clock. Full-time result? Something like 113–112.

I longed to play. As much as possible. There was a local

kids' team, the Calderwood Stars. The youngest team was
the Under-12s, which I was very keen to start playing for. The
thing was, I was just seven. The guy who ran the club was a
wonderful man called Albert England. One evening, I was
out on my bike, and I saw Mr England going into the
Calderwood Inn for a pint. I waited for him to come out, and
politely but enthusiastically approached him.

'Mr England,' I said. 'Can I play in your team?'

He looked me up and down.

'What age are you, son?'

'Seven.'

'You do realise we're an Under-12 team?'

'Aye.'

He smiled.

'You're a wee bit wee at the moment, son. How about next
year?'

'I'll be back,' I said, before riding away.

'Aye, I know you will, son.'

Just before my ninth birthday, I made my debut for
Calderwood Stars Under-12s. They were the best days, offering so many great memories. So many good friends playing
the game we loved. Mr England took the team, so did Gibby
Carmichael, Frank Gibson and my dad. To this day, I have
nothing but love and respect for the volunteers up and down
the United Kingdom who give up their time to take kids'
football teams.

That Calderwood Stars team were magic. Us kids wanted
to take on the world, but in the summer of 1974 in Germany,
just before my twelfth birthday, we had to make do with
watching our nation's football team trying it on our behalf.

I have memories of the previous 1970 World Cup in Mexico, the glorious colour, Gordon Banks's save against Pelé, England's untimely demise against West Germany, and the Germans' 4–3 defeat to Italy, an incredible football match. The tournament had hypnotised me into falling even more in love with football, and so four years on, to think that my own country, Scotland, would be competing against the very best – well, you can only imagine the excitement generated in my little corner of South Lanarkshire.

My mum loved having people over. Cups of tea, toast and sausage, all were on offer, and with the World Cup games, especially Scotland's, the living room was packed to the rafters. The games began, we beat Zaire comfortably two-nothing, but would ultimately regret not scoring more, and then we took on the Brazilians. The World Champions.

The atmosphere in the living room was electric. My own patriotism had been ramped up fully just weeks before, and believe it or not, it was at a rugby match. That February, my dad had taken me with his pals and a few other kids to Edinburgh to watch England at Murrayfield in the Five Nations. Once again us kids had stood outside local public houses, gorging on crisps whilst the men sank their pints.

In the stadium, Scotland found themselves one point down going into injury time, when Andy Irvine took a penalty kick from the far-right touchline, and it sailed over to win us the Calcutta Cup. Absolute bedlam. I will never forget it. The celebrations, the roar as the ball went over, the wild embraces, the inevitable pitch invasion, seeing the joy on the faces in the crowd. That was the moment I got it. That was the day my blood fully turned to tartan.

And so it was with a large amount of pride that we watched the team draw nothing-each with Brazil. We should have won it, by the way. I can see it now, Billy Bremner in the box. The ball not falling right for him, the great Leeds captain just unable to sort his feet out, and the chance is gone.

We were right to feel confident that summer of 1974. There was none of the hype that would send the squad off to Argentina four years later, but it was perhaps an even more talented group. Danny McGrain, David Hay and Kenny Dalglish, young members of Celtic's great new side, wee Jimmy Johnstone still dropping that shoulder and wreaking havoc, Sandy Jardine of Rangers. Great players plying their trade south of the border too. The likes of Bremner and fellow Leeds stars such as Peter Lorimer and Gordon McQueen; Denis Law, footballing royalty.

It was a team with potential, talent and experience, and so, going into the last group game against Yugoslavia, we all gathered in my parents' living room to watch our progress to the knockout stages. Us kids had got there early to get the sofa, but we were shocked when Yugoslavia went one up. Remember, this was our first tournament watching Scotland, so we had no prior experience of the excruciating plight that came with such summers.

The tension grew, but then an offering of hope, given to us by an early hero of mine, Joe Jordan. The big man scored late on, and the four of us kids on the sofa leapt so high (what felt like metres up) that when we all landed, the sofa broke with an audible crack.

My mum was seemingly very relaxed about the incident.

Citing normal youthful exuberance, she said, 'Not to worry. These things happen. More tea and toast anyone?' That was that. Or so I thought. Years later, fifteen years in fact, in 1989, Scotland drew 1–1 with Norway to ensure qualification for the 1990 World Cup. I had scored our goal and was feeling very pleased with myself, a mood made even better when a load of the old guard came into the dressing room to congratulate us.

Kenny Dalglish with his big smile, and alongside him, big Joe Jordan. They were patting us on the back, shaking our hands, saying well done, and then Joe turned to me.

'Great goal, Ally son, well done.'

'Thanks, big man,' I said.

'By the way, Coisty,' he said. 'I've just met a woman up the stairs, claiming to be your mother, wanting money off me for breaking her couch!'

All those years had passed, but my wee mum had remembered that moment when Joe's goal had caused the breaking of her family's couch, and now confronted with him, she suggested she be reimbursed. Magic.

Of course, as with so many years to come, the fairytale was over before any Happy Ever After. Big Joe's goal was not enough, and despite being unbeaten, the team were coming home. It was tremendously unlucky, but the side had perhaps been naive in not going at full pelt to score more against Zaire, a team who would later have a player booked against Brazil for running from his defensive wall and wellying the dead ball into the next town.

Scotland were coming home on goal difference, but us kids were full of pride in our players. We had also found new heroes. I certainly had. Gerd Müller, 'Der Bomber'; a stout centre forward who scored the winner in the final against the Netherlands, and caught my attention by doing so.

I had been playing a lot of my kids' football in midfield, but here was this guy, not big and tall like so many centre forwards we watched, yet able to make space for himself in the box and avoid big central defenders by outwitting them. This felt new. This felt like something I might be able to try.

The goal in that final is the perfect example. The ball was played in behind him, and eight yards out, he took a touch that kept the ball behind him, in space, away from defenders, and he was able to think fast, swivel, smash the ball into the ground and past the keeper, into the corner.

It was the first goal that made me think about technique. It was no classic, the ball didn't soar into the top corner, but it showed me how a striker can move, how they can deliberately manipulate things to create chances.

I got to see him play live. In 1976, when I was just thirteen, I headed to Hampden to see the European Cup final between Müller's Bayern Munich and a very cool St Etienne side, resplendent in their bright green shirts. It was the little striker who caught my eye the most that night, and I left the old stadium after Munich's 1–0 win with the wee man firmly on my mind.

I was always out in the park, practising, trying to swivel like him. Well, I wasn't going to try to impersonate the Dutch star Johan Cruyff, was I? Had I tried to copy the Cruyff turn, made famous that summer, I think I might have broken an ankle. No, it was Müller for me. That's the great thing about World Cups, especially for young people. The summer seems even more vivid. You remember the music you were listening to, what your friends were doing, the jokes you made, the girl you fancied, the clothes you wore.

We all wanted more, and thanks to Ally MacLeod's team four years later, we were once again the only Home Nations team to qualify. That feat had been secured in Liverpool. Scotland needed to avoid defeat to book their ticket to South America, and with the Welsh being sanctioned after some crowd trouble in Cardiff, their FA had chosen Anfield to host the game against us.

Big mistake. Huge. Anfield was invaded by Scots as tens of thousands of them made the trip, filling all four stands (including the Kop) in the ground, making it surely the biggest 'away support' in history. A McCoist was in the crowd too, as my sister Alison joined the mass exodus south and came home full of stories about the biggest party of her life.

The game itself was tight, but it turned on a controversial penalty awarded to Scotland after Joe Jordan drew a handball, shall we say, from the Welsh defender. It was slightly dubious, and I know a few Welshmen who, to this day, raise an eyebrow when the topic comes up. Kenny Dalglish put the game to bed with a header and the great Scottish commentator, Arthur Montford, summed it up perfectly when he simply said, 'Argentina, here we come.'

It was all about us. England, with all their powerful clubs competing in European Cups, were unable to join us and it felt sweet. Teams like Leeds, Liverpool and soon Nottingham Forest might be making European finals, but they were full of Scottish stars anyway, so it was a magic time when we felt we could really gloat, and we did.

Having left the pub near Hampden, my dad and myself, his pals and their lads all headed into the stadium, and there we found a party. A crazy going-away party full of Scottish bravado, mad Scottish optimism, and not yet delicate Scottish hope. The squad and their manager, dressed in greyish-blue suits (their kipper ties with knots big enough to keep the *QE2* moored – yes, Asa Hartford, I mean you) looking splendid.

'We're on the march with Ally's army . . .,' we sang. The players came onto the pitch one by one. Alan Rough, Kenny Burns, Graeme Souness, John Robertson, Archie Gemmill, Kenny Dalglish, Joe Jordan. Legends. Capable of winning the whole bloody thing. Right? Why not?

With each player coming from the tunnel to step onto the bus, the crowd were being revved up into a wild frenzy, until it was pandemonium. 'And we'll really shake 'em up when we win the World Cup, 'cos Scotland are the greatest football team!'

MacLeod had given his interviews after the draw had put his team into a group with Iran, Peru and the Netherlands (without Cruyff). This was on. We could beat them all, and according to our wild manager, we should expect third place at the very least. At Hampden, before setting off onto lined streets taking them to Prestwick airport and heading across the Atlantic to Argentina, MacLeod was interviewed by the newsreader, Trevor McDonald.

'Mr MacLeod, what will you do when you win the World Cup?'

The manager, without pause, smiled and said, 'Retain it.'

It was perhaps the single greatest line ever given by any

Scotsman, in any time. Us fans lapped it up. What a time. I lived and laughed within a community, I had the best of pals, a loving family, a love of football, and a love of music that enabled me to go to gigs to see some of history's greatest ever bands. Now I had hope that, maybe, just maybe, my country would top the world.

Yes, it had been raining that day, yes that rain had cut into our faces, but it couldn't erase the smiles from them. We are Scottish and as we say of rain up here, not to worry, most of it ends up as whisky, anyway.

three

STEAM TRAINS, TELEPHONES AND FOOTBALLERS

Us Scots love a good chat. A good 'blether' as they say up here. You can't beat it. Granted, it often involves a pub and a drink of some alcoholic description, but sitting with a group of like-minded people, chewing the fat, arguing the toss, making things right; it's very much part of Scottish life. Yes, to blether is to be alive. It's a wonderful thing.

History has it that it was over a right good Scottish blether that football changed forever. Picture the scene.

It's the late 1860s. The Queen's Park area of Glasgow. A group of men from as far away as Perthshire and the Highlands are sat around, and they begin to discuss how football, this game being played in England, might be bettered. Yes, the new game is becoming popular and the first set of laws have been drafted down south, and yes, an English FA has been formed, but what strikes these cerebral men as they get deep into it, is that the game of football lacks a certain degree of finesse.

They talk, and they talk some more, and what comes from arguably one of Scotland's greatest ever blethers is a new way of looking at football, a new way of playing it, and a style of football that would ultimately not only make the entire planet fall in love with it, but influence the greatest of footballing minds, including modern-day demigods such as Pep Guardiola.

Yes, I am suggesting, and I am not alone, that the beautiful game was born because of a good chat in the south side of Glasgow. English fans might sing 'Football's Coming Home', but us Scots know that whilst that home's structures might have been built in England, it received a lovely lick of paint and its more desirable soft furnishings north of the border.

The proof is there for all to see. After those men drew up their own set of laws, taking the game further away from the rugby-style sport the English had adopted with a combination of passing patterns and teamwork, Scottish players began to shine. The first international game between the two nations (between any two nations) was in 1872, but thereafter they became regular occurrences, with Scotland – and their nimble players adopting a more intricate style – the regular victors.

As England's Football League became more and more successful at the end of the century, it was Scottish players who greased the wheels, with all the big powerhouse teams such as Preston North End relying on Scottish talent. James Cowan, a quick half-back from Jamestown in Dumbartonshire, starred in the Aston Villa side that won five league titles and two FA Cups at the end of the nineteenth century, and was maybe the most famous of many who brought a certain way of doing things to a game that was now drawing in huge crowds.

The thing is with Scots, it is in our DNA to look at things, and wonder if we can make them better. Especially if we are told not to bother. It might be our size. A wee-man syndrome that sees individuals want to prove themselves and a country in general that has always strived to be much more than its population or geographical square mileage might otherwise suggest.

Tell us no, tell us that bigger men or bigger countries have got it covered, and a wee twinkle will begin to form in our eyes.

'Don't bother trying.'

'Here we go, give us a look. Okay, give us twelve months and come back. We'll have made it much better.'

Some scholars might even convince you that Scotland has played a huge role in shaping our modern world. Yes, that's right, there are plenty of cleverer people than me who can and will highlight Scottish influence in championing democracy, education and industry.

Famous names such as Alexander Fleming, Alexander Graham Bell and John Logie Baird are joined by other lesser known individuals. Dugald Stewart, an eighteenth- and nineteenth-century philosopher from Edinburgh; John McAdam, an Ayrshire engineer who is said to have invented modern road construction; or John Pringle from Roxburgh, said to be 'the father of military medicine' after his efforts fighting the French in 1743. All proud Scots changing the way people live, and proof that the list of what we have given the world goes way beyond Irn Bru (although, let's get one thing straight, Irn Bru is one of mankind's finest inventions).

In fact, Scots have invented plenty of things that I am particularly fond of. The bicycle, for instance. I love my bike and regularly get out on it, taking in the incredible scenery of Scotland's west coast. For that, I and so many others owe a thank you to Kirkpatrick Macmillan, a Dumfries-born black-smith who is credited with inventing the bicycle back in 1839.

There's penicillin, MRI scans, the flushing toilet, the phone, all given to the world with a splash of tartan. Fingerprinting. There's another one. Henry Faulds, a proud Ayrshire-man, credited with helping police forces every-where with his study of individual prints. Mind you, there will be a few unsavoury characters residing in small cells in certain parts of his country of birth, who might not be so quick to raise a glass to him.

What about Hamilton-born William Cullen, a professor at Edinburgh University who, in the eighteenth century, invented the fridge? Although, most people up here might argue that with weather like ours, it remains a pointless piece of equipment.

I recently discovered that it was a Scot who invented the ATM. The cash machine. Now this seems a strange one. The notion of an ATM seems to me to be every Scotsman's night-mare. Once the bank was closed, a true Scot was able to breathe more easily knowing that his hard-earned cash was simply not available. For a Scot to invent something that changed that? Were they some sort of masochist?

There's the steam engine, already in use but redesigned by Greenock's James Watt, who increased productivity by doing so and earned the name 'The father of the industrial revolution'. What Watt did was to take something invented by an Englishman and simply make it better, and that, you see, is exactly what the Scots did with football.

We took an invention, had a wee blether about it, refined it, and in time, it became not only the most watchable sport on the planet but also the most loved; and all of that was done with a degree of inventiveness of which the likes of Watt and Faulds would have been proud. The game became intricate, passing became everything, and football as we know it began to take shape.

Crowds flocked to matches (attendance records were repeatedly broken in Scotland) and English clubs in a flourishing new Football League looked northwards for the talent that would win them trophies.

Most of these pioneers were smaller than their English counterparts, relying on skill and cunning. I myself know what it is like to be told that you are too small to prosper, but Scottish footballers have always rebelled against notions that size matters. Look at the events at Wembley on the last day of March in 1928. Scotland came to London, not in the greatest form, but they went on to produce a performance and a result that has been talked about with boastful glee for almost a century.

England 1 Scotland 5. A win that labelled all those players in blue the 'Wembley Wizards' and created an almost mythical team. A team that for my generation meant being sat down and (whether we liked it or not) regaled with stories of their prowess. One of their greatest strengths, it seemed, was their height, or lack of it.

The front five consisted of James Dunn, Alex James, Hughie Gallacher, Alan Morton and Alex Jackson, and the latter, at five foot seven, was the tallest. Alex James got a brace, whilst Jackson got a hat-trick and the team were given a standing ovation by the English as they left the pitch. A standing ovation from Englishmen? Imagine how good you'd have to play to make that happen?

Two of the players particularly stood out, not just that afternoon but in the sport in general. Alex James of Preston North End and later of Arsenal, and Hughie Gallacher, then of Newcastle but soon a star at Chelsea, were arguably two of the five best players on the planet before the Second World War.

Both brought an abundance of skill to the game, James with his creativity linking defence and attack and Gallacher with an ability to beat a man (usually a much bigger man) with a drop of the shoulder and an unerring finish. Gallacher was a troubled soul, he would take his own life in tragic circumstances, but there was no doubting his cheeky character, which made him amongst the most popular players of his day.

The fact that his appearance at Wembley that afternoon was his first for a while having served a suspension for throwing a referee into a team bath, spoke of a man with a maverick streak to his nature. I'm led to believe that there was water in the bath and the referee could swim, so no real harm done.

Growing up at my dad's knee, listening to him, my Uncle George and their pals talking about football, you learnt about these great names, and so many others. After the war, my parent's generation in Scotland continued to marvel at how their compatriots, although small in numbers and still often in height, played their part in a now global game.

The players that helped Scotland reach the 1954 and 1958 World Cup finals and those that followed into the 1960s epitomised the Scottish game. Cheeky, skilful, creative, often diminutive but always brave, the Scots remained a major part of the English game too. Bobby Collins, the pocket-sized winger at Celtic, became an adored playmaking midfielder in England at Everton and then Leeds, where he helped shape Don Revie's great side. A Govanhill boy standing at five foot four on his tiptoes, Collins showed that wee-man syndrome in the English game and never shied away from the bloodcurdling physicality of the game in the 1960s.

Through that swinging decade in which I was born, and into the 1970s, every major team had their Scottish contingent. Liverpool under Bill Shankly, that proudest of Scots, owed much of their newfound success to two players, different in stature, but both brimming with Scottish drive. Ian St John, compact but fiery, and Ron Yeats, a colossal former abattoir man from Aberdeen, who led the club to untold success.

Paddy Crerand at Manchester United was the perfect foil for their Holy Trinity of Charlton, Best and Law; the latter arguably being the best our nation has ever produced. Leeds were full of them. Collins was followed by Billy Bremner, Peter Lorimer and his caber-tossing shots, Joe Jordan, all action and grit, and Gordon McQueen at centre-half. Spurs had won the double housing John White and Dave Mackay. Alan Gilzean would later join them from Dundee with wonderful and memorable effect.

Chelsea with Eddie McCreadie and the gliding Charlie Cooke, or Arsenal with Peter Marinello, a maverick striker. I could go on. Let's not forget Brian Clough's Nottingham Forest that won so much with the likes of Kenny Burns, a brilliant footballer able to influence a game from the back or the front, and John Robertson, a winger who might have looked like he'd raided his mum's toffee jar, but with the sweetest of left foots that conquered Europe.

Talking of conquering Europe, I was too young to remember the Lisbon Lions, who made Celtic the first British club to win the European Cup in 1967. For that eleven to have all been born within thirty miles of each other was incredible and what an array of Scottish talent. What a great team they were. Billy McNeil the centre-half and leader, Bertie Auld, Jimmy Johnstone on the wing, and my favourite Bobby Lennox, a goalscorer who caught my eye at a young age.

Another player whom the older guys would talk about at the time was Jim Baxter. The one-time Rangers playmaker was an incredible talent. A natural who was happiest with the ball at his feet. Jim had starred in the famous 3–2 win at Wembley in 1967, a game that crowned us Scots as World Champions. Jim produced the most iconic moment when, leading to the third goal, he nonchalantly moved forward whilst juggling the ball on his knees. Keepy-uppies at Wembley during a famous victory? No wonder so many of my dad's generation regarded him as the best they'd ever seen.

I got to know Jim later in life. We both played for Rangers and Sunderland, but in terms of natural ability, I'd suggest that's where the comparison ends. Jim was a warm, friendly man. He would have his own demons in life but he always approached me, asking me about my boys, how they were, if they were happy. I missed his heyday, but he remains a Scottish hero.

By the age of seven or eight, I started to have my own heroes. My dad had taken a liking to Third Lanark, the Glasgow club who had once known success but who went out of business and disappeared in 1967. My Uncle George and my mum were Rangers fans, they had to be because of my granny Jeanie, who adored the club, and might have wondered who my mum had married when he mentioned supporting Third Lanark.

There are some people in Glasgow who support other clubs in and around the city. The story goes that a stranger will walk into a pub. The locals will give them a bit of time, slowly get to know them and then they ask the question. 'What football team do you support?'

There might be a pause. 'Partick Thistle.'

Another pause. 'Yes, but are you Celtic Thistle or are you Rangers Partick Thistle?'

I guess you could say that my dad was Rangers Third Lanark.

I was just Rangers. My heroes were in the team who won the Cup Winners' Cup in 1972. Sandy Jardine and the captain John Greig, both great competitors. Colin Stein was probably my favourite. What a player Steiny was. His goal at Easter Road helped seal the title for Rangers in 1975. For that, eternal hero worship is guaranteed in many parts, but having been lucky enough to meet him and so many players of that era, what I love most is just how humble and lovely they remained.

Derek Johnstone caught my eye in the 1970 Scottish League Cup final when, aged just sixteen, he scored the only goal to beat Celtic at Hampden. He rose above Billy McNeil to score that day and, I can tell you, not many people rose above the captain they called Caesar. Big Derek had a fantastic career that saw him play both up front and at centre-back. He is an amazing man. One of the funniest I have ever met.

The big man won the Scottish Football Writers' player of the year in 1978. At the ceremony, he was there and was joined by the British prime minister, Jim Callaghan. Whilst making his acceptance speech, Derek took a pound note out of his pocket, dropped it to the floor, and said, 'Excuse me, Mr Callaghan, I think this must be yours, it's a falling pound!'

Everyone fell about, and later when the prime minister stood up, he congratulated Derek. He said how great he was, how funny he was, and told him that if he was ever in London, he must come by and say hello. Derek Johnstone immediately stood up and said, 'Sure, where do you stay?' The place broke up with laughter again.

Humour is very much part of the Scottish game. It has always been littered with characters, players who made us drool at their talent and fold over laughing at their wit. The fans love to laugh at a match, making up jokes and songs as they go – about players, referees, or themselves. A good laugh is a big part of Scottish life and a characteristic that buoys the nation's optimism.

I think the great Scottish players have all shown aspects of 'Scottishness' to help their game. Take the wingers. They have mesmerised and bamboozled full-backs for decades, and they've done so with a perfect mix of that inventiveness, cheekiness and a Scottish fondness for making mischief.

As a centre forward, I was in the best place to see some of these wingers close up, and also benefit from how deftly they beat players and got the ball into the box so that the likes of me could take the glory. I played with some great Scottish wingers. Pat Nevin was a great wide player, one able to use his head and who relished the creative side of the game.

All the great wide-men had that. A true, childlike enjoyment for getting on the ball, feeding off the excitement from the crowd, getting a spark from the one-on-one combat between them and often a nervous full-back.

At Rangers and with Scotland I was so fortunate to share a field with Davie Cooper. If someone asks me who was the best player I ever played with, Coops is always quickly into the conversation. He was the real deal. Actually, I say the real deal, but what makes people laugh is that when I tell them how good he was, I then add that he had no pace, couldn't head, no right foot, and certainly wasn't inclined to tackle, but what a great player.

Coops loved beating another player and would do so not with running, but with sleight of movement. He was old school. Coops had that lazy look, a drop of the shoulder or a swivel of the hips and that vital yard was his.

Young football fans have to look on YouTube for a goal we scored for Rangers in an Old Firm clash in 1986 at Ibrox. As ever, space was a rare and expensive commodity. No one is giving an inch, but Coops has had enough of all that. He gets on the ball, surrounded by midfielders not celebrated for their generosity of footballing spirit, and even more so when facing their city rivals.

One of them is Roy Aitken, a fantastic player, one who loved the Old Firm games, and wouldn't have minded if we'd decided to play them without a ball. The big man converges on Coops, denying space, hope and possibly air, but Coops has already beaten one man. So Roy hurls himself at him, but Coops lays it off with the outside of his left boot, whilst running to the right, and Aitken doesn't know what day it is as Ian Durrant runs through and scores. It must be the greatest eighteen-inch pass of all time.

It was typical Davie and after Ian scored, Coops stood with his arms outstretched waiting to celebrate with this new young talent, but the wee man ran right by him to wallow in the crowd's elation. Durrant took a lot of stick after that game. We should have all been praising him for scoring the winner against our big rivals, but instead we hammered him. 'Wee man, who the fuck do you think you are? How have you just custard-pied the legend that is Davie Cooper?'

The other winger that so epitomised Scottish wit and invention was Jimmy 'Jinky' Johnstone. I would have loved to have played with the wee man, but I was lucky enough to know him. A week before he passed away in 2006, I was able to visit him and whilst he was ill, that glint in his eye, that spirit along with that sense of humour, none of that could be extinguished. It was an honour to spend some time with him.

Jinky was the perfect Scottish winger. Small, with a lovely low centre of gravity, he could go either way, had the balance of a circus performer, and would weave in and out between full-backs who must have struggled to sleep after facing him, for feelings of sea-sickness. I love watching old clips of him. The way he played the game, it came with that childlike enjoyment. The wee man played with a smile, and he played so that those watching him smiled too.

Not that it was all smiles and laughter. Like all these wingers, Jinky had to face players who saw the wide areas in which they competed as gladiatorial arenas, where bloodshed was simply a consequence of their afternoon's work. Add the likes of Jinky to the equation and matters were going to get even more violent. There's only one thing a raging full-back hates more than a winger, and that's a winger who is embarrassing him in front of 50,000 people. These guys would have great chunks of flesh taken from their calf region, stud marks would be found on their stomachs, and elbow prints would reside on their dented cheeks.

That would not stop them, though. In fact, it seemed to spur wingers on. The good ones anyway. The likes of Jinky and Wee Willie Henderson, whom I watched as a boy at Rangers, would constantly show for the ball, demanding to be involved, often with their backs to goal, knowing that an attempted assault was to follow. I think they enjoyed it. The challenge was to receive the ball, avoid being cut in half, beat their assailant, and their team were away. If the assault was successful, they'd get up, wink and go again. That shows another Scottish trait, bravery, and these wingers – never the biggest of men – showed oodles of it.

Gordon Strachan certainly did. I love Strachs. He was the perfect example of a Scottish footballer bringing invention, wit and bravery (some might say bordering on foolhardiness) to a football pitch. Nimble and clever, Gordon would torment teams in Scotland whilst at Aberdeen in the early 1980s, but supporters too. This was a time when the connection between players and fans was very real, but that usually meant a possible fist upon a player's chin.

Never shy to wink at fans baying for his demise, Gordon would even go and warm up in front of the opposition supporters, including at Celtic. The wee man, at his peak, was somewhat of a wanted man, and that spilled over in 1980, when a fan ran from the Jungle at Celtic Park and tried to attack him. I think it was big Doug Rougvie who managed to pull the assailant off him, and whilst he was rightly arrested and banned, it is said that his fine (plus some add-ons) was paid for after a whip-round in the local Celtic pubs after the game. That's how much fans resented Strachan's ability to ruin their Saturday afternoons.

Strachan became more of a clever midfielder, playing with less width but just as much intelligence for the Leeds side that won the League Championship in 1992. There, he demonstrated that Scottish talent for on-field engineering. Working out the mechanics of a game and oiling a team's pistons.

There have been plenty of similar Scottish midfielders, able to dictate tempo, solve problems and ultimately create space and chances. I think of the likes of Paul McStay. Another brilliant player. And what a diamond of a human being. I don't think Paul was given the credit he deserved. Especially south of the border, where he could have walked into any of the top teams at the time. I don't mean to be unfair to the rest of his Celtic teammates, but it often felt as if he was taking us on single-handed in a period when we were very dominant, winning nine titles in a row.

Paul was that classic midfielder. Able to dictate the tempo of a game, a fantastic passer of the ball, brave and could look after himself, and I am 100 per cent positive he would have shone in the English top flight or even Serie A. No doubt about it. Funnily enough, my mum and his mum got on like a house on fire. They would meet at our international games and sit next to each other, and my mum would always say how much she enjoyed Paul's mum's company. That might have upset a few people at the time, Mrs McStay and Mrs McCoist from both sides of the tracks having a blether and a right old giggle together.

Talking of quality midfielders and right good giggles, I have to mention Ian Durrant again. I'm not sure I have ever come across a more talented young footballer. If you don't believe me, think of the others who have said the same thing. Graeme Souness and Ray Wilkins, to name a couple of class midfielders, who both remarked that they had not seen a better young professional than my pal Durrant.

What an absolutely magic player. As soon as he got into the first team at Rangers, the team he loved (he could walk to work from his house), we knew were dealing with someone special. He was so talented, so able to dominate games. Skilful, strong, courageous, a goalscorer, a midfielder or a number 10, he had the lot.

And then, in 1988, he got injured. His knee. Done badly by a tackle from Neil Simpson at Aberdeen. It was horrific. The worst tackle I've ever seen. It really could have ended his career. Probably should have. I think it would have ended the career of less mentally strong individuals, but I saw first-hand the effort and the single-mindedness that he put into getting back into the game.

He went to the United States and had revolutionary surgery. I believe he was the first athlete to have the Achilles tendon of a dead man placed in his knee. After Durrant's guinea-pig efforts, the procedure became popular with NFL players in the States.

With his new tendons, Durrant went to work. I would see him, first in each morning at the training ground, and I have never seen anything like his desire to be fit. On the weight machines, leg weights, pushing himself to make his quads strong again, and it worked. He got back and had a brilliant career as an international footballer, competing at the very highest levels of the Champions League.

I think he would say himself that he was no longer the box-to-box player he had been prior to the injury, but his overall game and his game intelligence meant he could continue to be the best player on the park most weekends. I do truly believe that, had it not been for his injury, he would have got a move to Serie A, the pinnacle of the game at the time, and we would have seen him wearing the colours of a Juventus or an AC Milan.

Durrant and I got on famously. I love the guy. He used to have terrible haircuts, but otherwise he was magic to have around. At the end of our careers, we spent a few seasons together at Kilmarnock and I have to say they were right up there with the best times of my life. Not much pressure, a great set of lads, and great football.

I was thirty-eight when I finished there, and whilst we had a constant laugh, we certainly put the work in. I'd like to think we dragged the boys along with us, taking pride in training and in ourselves. When you're older, you want the young lads playing with you to see that you were okay once, you want them to look at you and think, oh aye, that's why he scored a few goals, he's half-decent.

I broke my leg playing against Rangers and really should have packed it all in, but I was enjoying it so much and I am a bit of a stubborn bastard, so I insisted on getting fit and having one more year there. The legs were getting slower, but the mind remained sharp. Or sharpish. I remember one game at Motherwell with Durrant and myself looking more like *Dad's Army*, but showing a few young 'uns how it's done.

I am out on the right wing and Durrant is running with the ball, and he knows exactly the run I am going to make to receive his pass. The only problem is, the run these days takes a wee bit longer to make. I'm going to go outside the full-back, then inside, and I do, but slowly, until Durrant plays the perfectly weighted pass as usual, one touch, and it's a goal. We are celebrating and Durrant waits, stops, points to an imaginary watch on his wrist, and says, 'You all right for time, pal?' Magic memories.

What made Durrant such a great player was that game intelligence which so many of the Scottish greats have shown over the years, and for some of them, their greatness has gone well beyond our nation. Scotland has produced several players who can be regarded as amongst the greats of the global game.

Take Danny McGrain of Celtic. Truly one of the best right-backs of all time. He was still playing when I started out and whilst he had slowed down, his understanding of how the game worked was still better than anyone. If someone picks their all-time eleven and they tell me they have Danny at right-back, I am not going to argue. Yes, there might be the likes of Carlos Alberto, Cafu or Paul Breitner, but tell me you're going with Danny McGrain and you won't get any fuss from me.

And what about Denis Law? The Lawman is right up there as an all-time great of the game. A Ballon d'Or winner, an integral part of one of England's finest ever club sides and possibly Britain's greatest ever penalty box player, Denis remains a hero to many and it's vital that younger fans understand just how good he was.

Again, if you ask me to pick an all-time Scottish team, the Lawman is of course up front, along with Kenny Dalglish, and if you ask me to name an all-time British eleven, well, I'm keeping that same pair. What Denis and Kenny did for Scottish football, as European and even global superstars, may never be matched, and whilst I never saw Jimmy Greaves or John Charles play, I do think they remain the best strikers this island has ever produced.

Kenny, I got to see close up. What a pleasure that was. As a young striker, to train and watch and try to emulate him, it was everything. Not that emulating was ever going to be easy. Take one goal he scored against Belgium. It was 1982. I was twenty, trying to score a few goals at Sunderland, not yet called up into the full Scotland squad but watching this game on my telly, and suddenly I was observing greatness.

Graeme Souness clips the ball forward, Kenny has made a little run into the right-hand channel, receiving the ball with his back to goal. The Belgian defender follows him, but with a swivel, using the outside of his right foot, Kenny turns him and moves into the box, another slight body movement to lose the centre-half, and he curls the ball into the far top corner with his left foot. His arms are aloft and there's that big Dalglish smile.

I tell you, if I'd been on my mother's couch that night, I'd have broken it again.

Soon after, in training with the Scottish Under-21s, Paul Sturrock, another fine forward, spent some time trying to recreate the goal. The movement, the turn, the swivel and the shot. Suffice to say, we were out there for a good few hours, before we realised you cannot recreate a Van Gogh with mere crayons.

Kenny wasn't a quick player, but he beat opponents with quickness of thought, which in game intelligence bought him the yard he needed and then his unerring talent did the rest. Kenny had started in midfield at Celtic and you could tell that in there, he had learnt everything he needed to know about the game. Pure instinct.

Graeme Souness was similar but from a deeper role, and being in the hub of the match action, Graeme would dominate games because of his ability to know exactly what any given match needed. I played with him at Rangers and his best years were probably behind him, but what he continued to do was read the game, and act accordingly to turn it his team's way.

If the game had got frantic, he'd put his foot on the ball and slow it down, or if the team were under pressure, he'd maintain possession with short passes. When the game needed a shot in the arm, he became all action, or the crowd needed lifting, he would smash into a tackle. He may be remembered too much for doing the latter, but my word, he could play.

I guess the physicality of Graeme's game stands out and it is true that he could boast of another important Scottish trait, that of being hard as nails. Once again, Scotland can boast a long and proud history of players who could not only handle themselves on the field of play, but often saw that field as a personal battlefield. Dave Mackay springs to mind. The name alone sounds like it is made from concrete.

One of my heroes and later my manager at Rangers was John Greig, and he was one of the toughest players I had ever seen. To hear John rant about his hero, Dave Mackay, told me all I needed to know about the Edinburgh-born legend. There's that famous photo of him playing for Spurs against Leeds in 1966. Mackay had returned from a couple of breaks in his leg (a mere flesh wound to the big man) and it was said that he took offence to Leeds's Billy Bremner – another brilliant Scottish player but one who could start a row in a phone-box – to kicking him.

Now, Mackay went on to say that he wouldn't have minded if Billy had kicked the other leg, but it was because he was targeting the recently broken one that he lost his rag, and there's this image of him with a fistful of Billy's shirt whilst the Leeds man, his arms outstretched, is trying desperately to plead innocence before Mackay's knuckles introduce themselves to his upper lip.

It's a great photo, one that Mackay himself didn't like because he felt it made him look like a bully, which he wasn't.

I'm not sure anyone ever bullied Billy Bremner, but it sums up a time when for all the toughness of the game, there seemed to be a togetherness, and even these toughest of men valued some sort of integrity.

Fights could be followed by friendships. It certainly happened to me after I first met Ian Ferguson. Ian was the talk of the Scottish league at the time. A young and highly gifted forward at St Mirren, he was Rangers mad, lived near Celtic Park, but a real bluenose, and the talk was of him coming to Ibrox sometime soon.

We were at Love Street, and I was up against the big centre-half, Peter Godfrey. It was a physical game, and Ian, aged just seventeen, shouted to Peter, 'Hey, big man, stick it on him.'

I thought, hold on, and I shouted back, 'Why don't you get up here and stick it on me, ya wee fanny.'

To which he replied, 'Aye, I will.'

So, Ian came upfield and marked me. I was raging and crack, I smashed him in the jaw. He went down, he jumped up, mayhem ensued, players were everywhere, but the ref saw nothing and we played on.

Not long after, the Under-21s were training but the full manager, Andy Roxburgh, thought it a good idea if they joined us at Gleneagles for a dinner, and suggested us senior players leave a space for the young guys to sit next to us.

The doors open and I have my back to the guys walking in, but I say to Durrant, 'Keep an eye out, pal, let me know if that kid comes in running for me.'

Durrant begins to smile, and tells me that Ian is headed right for me.

'Aye, aye, here we go,' I say. 'This is it, round two!' Before I can turn, Ian has tapped me on the shoulder, and says with a cheeky smile, 'Is it safe for me to sit here?'

'You better believe it is, pal?' I say, and we have been best of friends ever since.

Less friendly have been the many Scottish centre-halves I have faced during my career, but whilst my ankles might disagree with my sentiments, I loved and relished playing against the big men. The way I saw it, if a central defender was kicking fuck out of me, I would accept it, because I knew, as night follows day, my central defenders were doing the same to their strikers.

I lived that side of the game. Centre-halves whispering all sorts in my ears, but I loved all the talk. I remember one, big John 'Yogi' Hughes at Celtic. We were always in each other's ears in Old Firm games and I would often successfully wind him up. One day the game got going and he said, 'Don't even talk to me, man. I have been told I am not allowed to talk to you, Coisty, I am going to ignore you all day.' That didn't stop me getting in his ear though.

There have been so many great Scottish centre-halves. Big Braveheart figures such as Colin Hendry, Alex McLeish and Richard Gough, willing to stick their head in where it hurts. They could all play, as could the likes of Dave Levine who had injury deprive him of a wonderful career, David Narey, and Paul Hegarty, who took on Europe's finest in the 1980s. Possibly the greatest of them all was Alan 'Jockey' Hansen, who was years before his time and easily one of the best European centre-backs ever.

It is strange that Jockey Hansen won only twenty-six caps for Scotland, but he played at a time when McLeish played every week at Aberdeen with Willie Miller, and such was the brilliance of their partnership, it became very hard for any national manager to break them up. Willie Miller was possibly the best eighteen-yard box defender I ever faced. He knew what a striker wanted to do, where he wanted to be, and he would block and block and block. He had that incredible moustache, which made him look like the villain in a silent movie, ready to tie a striker like me to the railway tracks, whilst twisting his 'tache and letting out a villainous laugh.

Whilst Scotland's almost ridiculous production of these truly great players has diminished somewhat over the past couple of decades, the country still continues to fight above its station, and wherever I go in the world, I am always so proud of the reactions I get from people about the footballers who have worn our famous blue jersey.

I can say I have watched Denis Law play and Jinky Johnstone play, I can say that I shared a football pitch with Kenny Dalglish, with Graeme Souness, with Davie Cooper and with Ian Durrant. Players such as Gordon Durie, Stuart McCall and Gary McAllister have been teammates, and have all shone at the game's highest levels.

We may be a small country, our population might be tiny, but when it comes to giving the world skilful and talented footballers, we are up there with the very best. And it's all thanks to a good old blether.

four

THE START OF SOMETHING

You have to hand it to Alan Rough; he let in some of the greatest World Cup goals ever scored. What a great guy Roughie is. One of Scotland's best keepers, over fifty caps for his country, nearly 600 games in our league, and one of the nicest, funniest, most self-deprecating men you will ever meet. When I think of the big man and our World Cup adventures, however, the image that comes to mind is usually him bending over to pick up the ball, having watched with us all as some international superstar has smashed it past him from some ridiculous range and into our rigging.

One of the most famous occasions was at the 1982 World Cup. The team's fixture against Brazil in Seville. Our team, on paper, has nothing to fear. Miller, Souness, Hansen, Strachan, Robertson; some of Britain's finest. However, there's one wee problem, the opposition's team sheet.

Socrates, Serginho, Oscar, Eder, Falcão, Zico; some of the universe's finest.

To be fair, as the game gets under way, Scotland are holding their own, battling in midfield, trying to get their widemen in the game and seemingly coping with the Andalusian evening's 30-degree heat. Then Scotland make their first mistake. They score. David Narey, Dundee United's brilliant defender, ventures forward, finds some space and sends the ball into the top corner with what the BBC's Jimmy Hill calls a 'toe-poke'.

For fifteen minutes, Scotland are beating the tournament favourites. Everyone back home has gone full Ally MacLeod and, for those fifteen minutes, we're winning the whole bloody thing. Soon though, the Brazilians begin to buzz like yellow hornets whose nest has been (toe-) poked. On thirty-three minutes, the great Zico sets himself for a free kick, the defensive wall stands true, but are deemed redundant by the whip and curl that sends the ball whizzing past a static Roughie and into the top corner.

With that goal, the Brazilians start to turn it on, and are pinning our boys back. Moments after the equaliser, a foray forward has Falcão passing to Socrates, Socrates laying it on to Eder, Eder finding Zico, Zico laying it back to Falcão, whose goal-bound strike is tipped over by Roughie. Legend has it, that when the players gathered for the corner and were congratulating their keeper, Roughie said, 'Thanks, lads, but I was still going for Zico's free kick!'

That is one of my favourite stories ever, and says a lot about the way Scotland have somehow always managed to find themselves up against giants of the game, legends who for various reasons have been moved to make our lives a misery with moments of brilliance.

Zico's goal that night was followed by one apiece from Oscar, Eder and Falcão. All of them contenders for goal of the century. You also have to add Gazza's piece of mind-bending skill in our Euro '96 clash with England at Wembley. Once again, it's as if we had provoked genius.

It all started back in 1978 though. Moments after our own dabble with tournament immortality. Our last game in that World Cup was against the Dutch. Due to a couple of lapses in concentration in the opening two group games, Scotland needed to beat the Dutch by three clear goals, and at 2–1 up, Nottingham Forest's Archie Gemmill picked up the ball, beat a man, dropped a shoulder, nutmegged a defender and in a moment that is right up there in Scotland with the birth of Robert the Bruce, lifted the ball over their keeper and suddenly, it was back on. It was arguably the greatest goal of all time. Scrap that, it *is* the greatest goal of all time, and if the rest of the country was anything like my mother and father's living room after that, the whole place was going berserk.

The elation lasted three minutes and twenty-seven seconds, and then the Dutch legend Johnny Rep picked up the ball, strode forward and from what felt like sixty yards, lashed the ball into the top corner of Roughie's goal. Another legend, another stroke of genius, and once again, it was time to go home. If we had all given MacLeod and his team the send-off of a lifetime, they came home to emptier streets, but looking back, they were simply setting a precedent. At major tournaments, Scotland just have a tendency to bring out the best in the best, and on numerous occasions tend to go out in a blaze of madness.

By the time Ally's army had retreated from Argentina, my own callow career had been showing signs of life. For much of that I can thank a great teacher I had at Hunter High School by the name of Archie Robertson. He took the school team and taught chemistry. He was immaculate at both. Like the subject he taught, Mr Robertson was methodical, thoughtful and sometimes explosive.

Always well turned out, slicked-back hair, a shirt and tie, he was a lovely, passionate man. He had also played hundreds of games for Clyde, winning five Scotland caps and representing the country at the 1958 World Cup in Sweden, and to be around a former pro was massive. To be coached by him was a blessing. He was old school, so you didn't mess about. He was always encouraging and without having favourites, he saw some promise in me and would take me aside, but never to the detriment of another student.

It was like having a father at school, a perfect preparation for a young footballer who one day would work with the likes of Jock Stein and Walter Smith, and whilst the periodic table he taught me might have slipped from my mind, his work ethic, his elegance and his respectfulness have stayed with me. He was also a stickler for punctuality, a trait I am not famous for, and he might give me one of his stern looks today if he knew of my capability for being late.

Mr Robertson didn't talk much about his own football career, and his ill-health, which sadly took him from us early in 1978, meant he was not able to play much, but he was a fine teacher of the game. Rather than simply overseeing matches in which we all tried to shoot and score, he worked on bettering our technique and what are now known as 'patterns of play'.

For instance, instead of letting us take a corner, he would stop play and work on short-corner routines. Ironic really, given that Mr Robertson had scored straight from a corner for Clyde in the 1955 Scottish Cup final against Celtic. Clyde won the Cup that year and he would win a second winners' medal in 1958. I was proud to know Mr Robertson, he made me better and we all were so sad when he died.

With his guidance, my football had improved and I caught the eye of St Mirren's young manager, Alex Ferguson. As I mentioned earlier, Ferguson stayed in East Kilbride back then and he used to take me and another young striker called Stevie Cowan up to Paisley, so we could train with the kids whilst he worked with the first team. Alex was great with us, always asking how everything was going, but one day he took me aside and told me he thought I was too small, and he was signing Stevie instead.

It was a blow, but soon I was playing for Fir Park Boys, essentially Motherwell's youth team, and the club would offer me schoolboy forms. I was there with Gary McAllister, who became an immediate pal of mine and he was a pleasure to play with, even back then. It was great at Fir Park. Very professional. We had the tracksuits, proper training, everything a boy needed, and it did feel like a path into the pro game. There was an unfounded rumour that I turned down Rangers, but that's not true. They sent scouts to watch me a few times, but no offer was ever made.

The Motherwell manager at the time was a lovely big bloke called Roger Hynd. Roger was Bill Shankly's nephew, had played centre-half for Rangers, and was a very nice man, but I was also being watched by a St Johnstone scout called Alex McClintock. Alex knew two things and he moved quickly. He knew that the tempting Rangers were watching me, and that I didn't fancy the schoolboy forms being offered by Motherwell.

The S-forms didn't sit right with me. I wanted to play first-team football, and McClintock was adamant when he visited my house to talk to me and my parents that this would happen at St Johnstone. 'Forget all that schoolboy nonsense,' were his words. I was interested, not because I was arrogantly presuming that I could walk into the team, but I felt being in and around professionals was the better route for me. So it was that I signed with the Perth club on St Andrew's Day in 1978, on semi-professional forms.

If it was an education I wanted, that was what I got. My early games were with the reserves, but an early run-out for the first team against Raith Rovers woke me up to the more physical side of things at that level. I was up against a mountain of a centre-half, a guy called Donald Urquhart. A solid pro. Seasoned. Not me, though. I was being Jack the lad, my youthful naivety telling me to fight his physicality with cockiness.

I was basically a teenager giving it the big 'un. I was mouthing off, doing step-overs, and winking at the big man. Soon, though, I wasn't. The ball got played up the line, I made the run, big Donald went with me and, crack. He punched me square on the chin and I was out for the count. Next thing I knew was smelling salts, the trainer was slapping my face, my jaw was in bits, and the big centre-half was just getting on with things. No cameras, no action from the referee, and certainly no remorse. The game finished and Donald strolled over, shook my hand, no eye contact and walked off.

On the train home with my dad, he had a simple line of questioning. 'Did you learn anything today, son?'

'Aye.'

'What did you learn?'

'Respect.'

'Good.'

That was that. I might have been raging at what had happened, I was probably upset at being shown up, but my dad had seen it all and rather than being irate at the guy hitting me, or that no action was taken, he knew that Donald Urquhart was teaching me some vital lessons.

The manager when I signed for the Saints was Alex Stuart, but he was replaced in April 1980 by Alex Rennie, who played a big part in changing the way I played. Stuart had played me in deeper roles, as an attacking midfielder, but it was Rennie who saw me as an out-and-out striker, and stuck me up front with his centre forward, John Brogan.

Brogie was a legend. A goalscorer, a fantastic player who ran defenders ragged. He was clever. He knew what space to attack and being from Hamilton, not far from East Kilbride, we hit it off right away, on and off the pitch. They were a great set of lads. We had Johnny 'Dingy' Hamilton, a cracking wee midfielder who provided the guile. He had played for Hibernian and Rangers, and it showed.

As well as Dingy's cuteness, we had great delivery into the box from John Pelosi on one flank and Tam McNeil on the other. Us strikers had plenty of service and Brogie was especially apt at taking advantage. I hope Brogie won't mind me suggesting that his finishing was about power over finesse, and on many occasions the ball was smashed into our opponents' net. I loved Brogie, what a strike partner.

I got my big break next to him, and an early taste of fame, thanks largely to the good old Scottish weather. One Saturday, the weather was bad, even by our standards, and nearly every game was off. Rumour had it that it was so cold, even the curling games were off.

Ours at Muirton Park, against Berwick Rangers, was one of the few to survive. The STV cameras were in town to show a curling match at the Perth Ice Rink, and they were told to decamp to our ground to cover St Johnstone vs Berwick. We were great that day, we won 6–2 and I scored four. That night, I was on the box, the great Arthur Montford was talking all about our 'vintage' performance and he mentioned me. It was surreal, I can still picture the sports jacket he was wearing, and it was my first taste of television notoriety. The nation would have forgotten me by the Sunday morning, but it was a big moment in the McCoist household.

Jock Stein getting the national team job in 1978 was a massive deal for Scotland. His achievements at Celtic had made him and his team of locals that won the European Cup in 1967 immortal and to have the big man in charge of the national team (especially as he was taken from a very short stint as the boss at Leeds in England) was special to us all.

Jock was a man that crossed the deepest divides in the Scottish game. The likes of Jock, Walter, Billy McNeil and

John Greig were men who were wholeheartedly adored everywhere they went. With Jock at the helm, I felt sure that the country, still possessing so many world-class footballers, could go one step further than the 1974 and 1978 World Cups and progress to the second group stage.

You could argue that the 1982 squad that Jock took to Spain was the best of the three so far. Souness, Alan Hansen and Dalglish were serial winners in the English game and already multiple European Cup conquerors. Gordon Strachan, Willie Miller and Alex McLeish were tearing up Scotland's Old Firm domination at Aberdeen. Narey and Paul Sturrock were doing the same at Dundee United. Alan Brazil and John Wark were part of Bobby Robson's exciting UEFA Cup-winning Ipswich side and the likes of Steve Archibald and John Robertson were amongst the most talented forwards playing south of the border.

Defensively too, the squad was packed with a combination of experience (Danny McGrain was there!) and budding talent, but it was the goals against column that eventually saw the team underachieve, and the two goals conceded in a 5–2 win over New Zealand plus a Keystone Cops goal given away against the Soviet Union in a 2–2 draw ultimately cost Jock and his team.

By the time Willie Miller and Alan Hansen were running into each other in Malaga, I was playing my football in England, for Sunderland. I had scored some goals for St Johnstone, but it was what I had learnt about being a professional footballer that was my biggest take from life at Muirton Park. Being there totally vindicated my decision not to sign S-forms with Motherwell, and being around these seasoned pros was perfect, watching how they went about their business whilst having the time of my young life.

But with those goals came interest from other clubs, and it struck me that a club like St Johnstone were always going to cash in, and that meant doing the best deal for them. The clubs in England looking at me included Wolverhampton Wanderers, Spurs and Sunderland. Rangers showed an interest too, which obviously pricked up my ears, but with the Ibrox club offering £315,000, and then Sunderland offering a firm £400,000, it became obvious that I was being 'manoeuvred' to try my luck south of the border.

I don't blame St Johnstone, they had to look out for themselves, and the difference in money was substantial. I liked the people at Sunderland, the move was not too far from home, and whilst Rangers would have been a very attractive prospect for me, it wasn't going to happen. Not yet. In 1981, after all, there was no such thing as 'player power'.

My two-year spell at Roker Park, whilst nowhere near good enough in terms of the number of goals I scored, was a fantastic continuation of my footballing education and I returned to Scotland that bit older and a considerable bit wiser.

It had come to my attention in 1983 that Rangers were interested in signing me, and as much as I liked Sunderland, I felt I could get my career on a firmer footing back home. My Rangers hero, John Greig, was now manager there, and when we spoke on the phone, he had one question, 'Do you wanna come up the road, son?'

The answer was yes, but I was skint, and he had to lend me twenty quid for the petrol to make it up the A74. We met in a hotel and things happened very quickly. Greigy was every-thing I hoped he would be, the deal was done and I had to make a phone call.

My wee granny, Jeanie Agnew, was a massive Rangers fan. I loved her to bits. She was a typically Scottish maternal figure in our lives. A powerhouse, small in stature but massive in heart, humour and love. She spoiled all her grandkids, but she was particularly attentive to my sister and me. My dad had lost both his parents, and Jeanie knew that she was our only grandparent, so an extra pack of sweets or a bit more of a fuss might be reserved for us McCoists. Not that her love for the others wasn't on show, it always was, but she had this way of noticing small details and making a massive difference.

Her love for her family was matched only by her love for Rangers, and so when Greigy and I had shaken hands (and he had got his £20 back), the only phone call I wanted to make was to Jeanie. Straight into a phone box, I knew her number by heart (I still do!), 10p in the slot, and I listened as she screamed in delight at the news.

Being at Rangers was wonderful, albeit initially during a time of transition at the club. I managed to score some goals and I hoped to get on Jock Stein and the national team's radar soon. I had certainly learnt a bit from my teenage days at St Johnstone, especially when it came to coping with bloodthirsty centre-halves.

If Donald Urquhart had taught me about respect, another big fella at Raith Rovers called Allan Forsyth had educated me on the art of kicking lumps from my ankle. Alan was known as 'Big Elvis', I presume because he liked the 'King of

Rock 'n' Roll', but when it came to physical defending, he was always on my mind.

Playing at St Johnstone, Allan had kicked me all over the park, and one day, now with Dunfermline, he came to Ibrox and it was clear that his plan was to do exactly the same again. It was a cup game, and Dunfermline were winning 2–1. A big shock was on the cards but we equalised, and then I scored a late winner. I had slid in at the back post, and as I was on the floor with the ball in the net, Allan had one thing in mind. He came in very late and went to give me a clump. I was prepared, though. I saw it coming, swerved, and popped up with a big smile on my face. 'Two years is a long time in football, big man!' I shouted. He loved it and after the game in the players' bar, we had a few pints and a right laugh about the old days.

With goals being scored regularly, Jock picked me for the national squad trying to qualify for the 1986 World Cup in Mexico. I was ecstatic. Suddenly I was in the company of greatness, Jock himself, a titan of the game, and his assistant Alex Ferguson, a giant in waiting, and to be around players such as Kenny Dalglish, Graeme Souness, Roy Aitken and Willie Miller was everything a young player could ask for.

Jock didn't give me my first cap, but I kept joining the squad and to me, that was enough then. To be training with these guys, to be listening to Jock's thoughts on the game and taking in his and his senior players' methods, was like being at the best of footballing universities.

Jock had me there to have a look at me, but also to see what I was made of and so that I could learn. The team meetings and being on the bus with the players, training with them, hearing about tactics, I took it all in. I was never left frustrated by Jock. I wanted to walk before I ran, and those squads were everything to me.

So was Jock Stein. I never got very close to him, but I observed him all the time, soaking in his genius. So the night that Scotland went to Cardiff, and got the draw we needed to progress in qualification for the World Cup, remains the saddest for all of us who knew and loved him.

I wasn't there that night, but went from celebrating my brilliant teammate Davie Cooper's late, pressure-busting penalty to draw us level, to hearing the news that the big man had been taken ill, and then the unbelievable report that he had gone. It was unbelievable because Jock seemed indestructible and he had a godlike stature. When Bill Shankly called him 'immortal', he was not kidding. Even forty years later, Jock Stein's death doesn't seem real. His presence is certainly ingrained in the nation's psyche.

The nation's football team had to move on quickly, and it was Alex Ferguson who took the team through a play-off against Australia, and on to the World Cup. Part of that preparation was several warm-up games, and it was in one against the Netherlands in Eindhoven that I won the first of my sixty-one caps.

I remember it like it was yesterday. Putting on that blue shirt, walking out, thinking of my parents and my friends, and how we had watched endless Scotland games and tournaments. We actually played well that night in Holland, but despite having a number of chances (looking back I could have scored a couple), and having two stonewall penalties turned down, we only drew 0–0. The Dutch had big names such as Hans van Breukelen in goal, Ronald Koeman, Danny Blind and Jan Wouters, players who would help win their country the European Championships two years later, but we were the better team, and it gave me a taste of football at the highest level. A taste I wanted more of.

That game in Eindhoven was the last friendly prior to the squad being named, and if I hoped I had done enough to get the nod, my hopes were quickly dashed. Having told me I was too small to sign for St Mirren, around nine years earlier, it was Alex Ferguson who had to break some bad news again.

In the spring of 1986, things were changing at Rangers; the manager Jock Wallace was leaving and behind the scenes Graeme Souness was planning his imminent appointment. I came into Ibrox one day and was told to get upstairs to see Jock. I walked into his office and could hear that he was having a heated conversation over the phone, and it was about me. After a minute or so, Jock turned to me and said, 'It's Alex, he's not taking you . . .'

I took the phone and Fergie explained to me that it was too soon for me, but – and this lifted my spirits – there was a possibility that someone could drop out and I should keep focused, because there still might be a chance. A few days later, Kenny Dalglish pulled out of the squad. Here we go. Was this my chance? No, Steve Archibald got the nod.

I was distraught, but it didn't last and as I sat down to watch the games that summer, I knew I had won only one cap, and I realised that if you looked at the quality of the strikers ahead of me in that squad, it was always going to be difficult. Kenny didn't go, but he was replaced by Archibald, the

Barcelona centre forward. They also had Graeme Sharp, Everton's striker and one of the best in the English First Division; Charlie Nicholas at Arsenal; Frank McAvennie, who that season had been unbelievable at West Ham; and Paul Sturrock, who was leading the line for a fantastic Dundee United team.

In the end though, even with that list of strikers, goals were hard to come by in Mexico, and having scored only one against Germany through Gordon Strachan (having lost 1–0 to Denmark), the side needed to win against a dirty Uruguay side, who despite having a player sent off in the first minute, frustrated us and, once again, it was the end.

I was thousands of miles away, but as I watched along with everyone else, seeing the team search forlornly for a goal, I was desperate to be there, to be part of a World Cup squad. That team's dreams were all over, but maybe mine were just beginning.

five

ANOTHER WEEK
OF DREAMING

SOMETIMES you have to laugh . . .

It is 1990, Scotland have qualified for another World Cup, and we're feeling good about ourselves in our picturesque base-camp in the exotic seaside town of Portofino on the Italian Riviera. It is one of our better squads. The likes of Richard Gough, Paul McStay, Roy Aitken, Alex McLeish; a very good set of lads.

Our qualifying group included Norway, Yugoslavia and France. We beat the French two-nothing at Hampden and Mo Johnston got both goals. (I scored one as well but it was chalked off for offside.) Mo and I played a lot together in those qualifying rounds and I scored the goal against Norway that clinched qualification.

We have that great squad, but I am confident that Mo and I will start the opening match against Costa Rica. The night before the game, the manager Andy Roxburgh and his assistant Craig Brown, for reasons known only to themselves, decide to name the team in sections. The keepers will be called to a room, told who was playing, then the defenders, then the midfielders and finally us forwards.

It comes to our turn. That's myself, Mo, Alan McInally, Gordon Durie and Robert Fleck. Andy and Craig are at a desk and us five are sat in front of them. It feels like a job interview and I am probably sat there amongst my four pals with the demeanour of a man who has already got the job. I'm pretty sure my name is going to be called imminently.

Andy is talking away, explaining his plans, he's going to go 4–4–2, he names the team, and then comes to the strikers. What I hear is, 'I'm gonna start with MoandAlly.' It comes out as one word. 'MoandAlly'. That'll do me. That's what I thought he'd say. Thank you very much. Time for my first World Cup start.

I am sat there, looking slightly smug. Andy is chatting away. I have a wee smile on my face. I notice Craig Brown looking at me with a strange expression. What I haven't realised is what Andy had said (albeit in a very fast and confusing way) was, 'I'm playing Mo and McInally.' So I'm sitting there, smugly contemplating my World Cup finals debut, with a grin I'm struggling to conceal, all the while I have completely misunderstood him. Craig is looking at me and he must be thinking, fuck me, Coisty's taking this hell o'er well.

I'm tuning into every word, listening to the boss's words of intent, but then the penny drops, he meant Alan bloody McInally and I'm benched. I've gone from scoring the goal against Norway that gets us to Italy, to not playing. Fuming. I'm absolutely fuming. Devastated. I stay professional for the rest of the chat, but then I am off, out the room and up the stairs.

To make things a million times worse, my roommate for the duration of that summer is Alan McInally. I'm away to the room, and as you do, when you're pissed off, you phone your dad. I'm sat on my bed, the bedside lamp is on and my dad is on the phone. He can hear my devastation, the many swear words coming out of my mouth give that away a wee bit, and he's trying to calm me down.

'Relax, son, calm down, Ally.'

How can I calm down? Instead I am ranting away.

'That bastard has dropped me.' All of that. Of course, it's all about me. At this point the team can do one, my head is battered and Dad is getting all the anger. And then, mid-rant, I hear someone coming out of the corridor lift and walking towards the room, and they're singing.

They're singing 'Flower of Scotland', but in the style of a drunk Scotsman. It sounds like Vic Reeves's club singer. 'Oooooh Floooower ooof Scooootland . . .' It's that bastard McInally. He's belting out the national anthem. I tell my dad, 'I'll have to go, I'll phone you back.'

'Just stay calm,' he says one more time. The phone goes down and into the room, still singing, walks Alan. I pick up my wee crossword book as I am thinking, I can't look at this bastard, and I start to pretend to be doing it. So I am sat on my bed, pretending to do this crossword, and he marches right in, 'Oooooh Floooower ooof Scooootland . . . When will weeeeee seeeeeee . . .'

He turns, he looks at me in my bed, he stops singing, and he says, 'Hey you.'

I don't want to look at him.

'Hey, you . . .' he says again.

I lift my eyes from the crossword, and I slowly turn to look at him.

'What is it?' I say.

There's a pause.

'Get tha' fuckin' light oot, some of us have a game tomorrow.'

Honest to god, it is one of the best lines I have ever heard, and suddenly I am on the floor laughing, and the pain and the anger have disappeared. Alan then starts pushing it. He's gone to his bag, pulled out his boots and asked if I can give him a hand cleaning them. He is hilarious, and I have gone from sheer despair to crying with laughter and thinking life is no' bad after all.

That's the thing. Sometimes you just have to laugh, and the days after that mauling by the Germans in the opening game of Euro 2024, there is little else us Scots can do. If Alan had come into the room and been solemn, and tried to console me, I'd have gone off my head at him. The only way to deal with the situation was to make a joke of it. Alan made quite a few jokes to be fair, going in a bit two-footed, but it worked. Absolutely magnificent.

It is that memory, the thought of the big man walking into the room and making me howl with laughter in my darkest hour, that arms my defences, because I know I am in for a lot of stick from English colleagues revelling in the Germans having taken my country's football team apart. I'm not looking for sympathy, and a glance at social media clearly underlines the revelry that is going with the result.

I do not want a cuddle, I want a 'By the way, how shite were you?' and that's what I get. Fortunately the game was on a Friday night, so I am spared any immediate exposure on the talkSPORT breakfast programme, and by the time I am on it the following Monday morning, the English guys such as Jeff Stelling and Gabby Agbonlahor are far more concerned with their own country's stuttering start the night before.

To be fair to the likes of Jeff, they want Scotland to do well. There is, of course, a knowing nod to how bad Scotland were, but they would rather we turn this around and do well. Then you get the likes of Jason Cundy and Jamie O'Hara. Two guys slaughtering us from London. They are magnificent, they make me laugh, but they are probably the two main reasons that Scots want the England football team to fail. I am pleased they have stayed in the London studio, as bumping into either or both of those two characters might wipe the smile from even *my* face.

Leaving Munich, I can see I am not the only one still smiling. Amongst the hangovers, and the odd kilted individual who has set up bed on the city's comfy pavements, there is a sense of, 'On we go.' When you come off a sore one like the German result, I think it's all you can do. I also think it's in the blood.

I have mentioned the Scottish rain before and I think it plays its part here. If you spend your whole life opening the curtains of a morning and seeing incessant, horizontal rain, you are prone to taking life's hits with a degree of stoicism.

It's sink or swim, and in the face of constant adversity, we choose the latter.

No one had us to beat the Germans, a draw would have been a minor miracle and sure, we would have liked a better performance, but now it is a two-game tournament for us. A tournament in which the format means that one win will give us half a chance, whilst a draw and a win will see us through. Switzerland await and then Hungary, two good sides, but two beatable sides. So, I leave Munich, headed for Stuttgart to cover Denmark vs Slovenia, and I am buoyed by that fighting spirit. A spirit that is epitomised by Denmark's Christian Eriksen, who scores a wonderful goal in the game, just three years after suffering his on-field cardiac arrest. If that doesn't tell you how people can bounce back, nothing will.

The game itself isn't a classic, but after going a goal down, the Slovenians show just how good and how up for it the smaller nations are going to be in this tournament. They really have a go at the Danes, equalising, and they should possibly have won the game.

I very much enjoy doing the co-comms. The big games are special, of course they are, commentating on the best teams and the best players in the world is an absolute pleasure, but I also like watching lesser known talent, and there is a lot to learn. I think the days of working on these games and not knowing too much about these players are very much over. You need to be armed with information, to do some home-work and be able to tell something new to the audience, who nowadays have so much info at their fingertips.

To be able to do that, we have to rely on an incredible stats team, and at ITV, a guy called Joel Miller deserves a mention, because he and his colleagues are at a different level. I am old school, I ask for a printout of his stat pack. Most have it emailed to their phones or tablets, but I like a physical one printed out for me so I can add some notes of my own in pen. Joel provides these packs that give us so much info on the players. Their caps, their goals, who they play for and with, and (this is key) how to say the name phonetically. That is a godsend, I can tell you.

We also have a WhatsApp group, with all the commentators and the stats guys. We can use it to get in-game stats too. Eriksen scores for Denmark, and ping, our phones are going with additional info about when he last scored, or something relative to what the viewers are seeing.

Of course, it can't all be data and statistics. An audience wants more. I want to explain things that maybe some viewers won't have noticed. Take the Eriksen goal again. I cannot simply say, 'Eriksen hits it and it's gone in.' I have to get the fact across about the run he's made, and, as a striker once myself, I'll try to go into detail about how great the flick is to him, but also how difficult and perfect his first touch on his chest is. How he has to move his bodyweight onto his left-hand side, so that he can cut across the ball with his right foot, keep the ball down and therefore hit it into the bottom corner.

It's a beautiful goal and I am hellbent on getting across that if he had met the ball straight on, he would very likely have missed. I get a real thrill from analysing the game that way, especially goals.

It is on to Cologne for Scotland's second game, five days after the Germany defeat. Travelling around this magnificent country is a pleasure. Fans from all over Europe mingling, drinking, laughing and loving football together, whilst being hosted and adored by the Germans, underlines what a celebration of football these tournaments should be.

There might have been a few television and social media clips of some trouble involving various sets of fans, but what I am witnessing is a festival of football that involves a lot of beer, yes, but a mingling of cultures and a backdrop of humour. There is a healthy camaraderie amongst fans and locals alike, and the atmosphere I'm sampling is one of real footballing empathy and fun.

It's no different in the beautiful city of Cologne. The vast numbers of Scots who had been in Munich have been added to here in the city on the Rhine. Cologne is a wonderfully cultural place, housing museums, galleries, and the most perfect cathedral. It also has historic links to perfume, and being the birthplace to Eau de Cologne there are plenty of references to its fragrant past.

With that, you would anticipate the city has a permanently pleasant whiff about it, but I can report that with the arrival of 150,00 Scottish folk onto its beautiful streets, many of whom have been drinking beer for a week and unable to shower for several days, the place now has what we might call a muskier scent in the air.

The first thing I do after I get off the train is drop my bags in the hotel and head to the cathedral. It's stunning. I am on my own for a night, so I take myself around the place and my jaw is agape at its magnificence. I am now at an age where I focus on things that I find beautiful, and my time in and around the cathedral reminds me of my old mum, bless her, who used to note the same thing. I am in awe of the place, and it is a fantastic afternoon and evening spent enjoying its beauty.

Soon though I am not alone, as I head out onto the streets and get lost amongst the throng of familiar-sounding accents and the Tartan Army, who have once again made a German city their own. The locals have that look on their faces, the usual combination of delight, amusement and sheer bafflement at this vast array of individuals, who fill their hitherto calm streets with song, laughter and merriment.

These days I tend to wear a baseball cap, more in the hope of covering a receding hairline than the hope of celebrity anonymity. Add to that I wear glasses, and so as I sit having a pint, wearing both, I have guys coming up to me and saying, 'By the way, Coisty, your disguise isn't working.' I have to explain that I need these glasses to see and if I wanted to be hidden, I would have worn a false nose and moustache.

The guys are brilliant. They always approach me with a smile, wanting a laugh and a blether, and I am happy to join them for both. And it's not just my fellow compatriots who are taking an interest. Prior to one game, I am sat in the hotel and this local is looking at me. I'm thinking, this is Germany, there's no way he recognises me. I walk past him, nothing, and I go to the desk to get my key, turn and there he is, standing right in front of me.

He points to me. 'You.'

I say, 'Yeah.'

'You . . .' he says, and he takes out his phone to show me a YouTube clip.

So, I am thinking here we go, he's a football connoisseur, a man who knows his Golden Boot winners. He's seen the red card I got against Cologne in 1988 in the UEFA Cup, or he was impressed with my performance against Germany in the 1992 Euros. In fact it was neither. Instead he pulls out his phone, puts on YouTube and shows me that viral AC/DC clip: 'You cannae beat a bit of AC/DC.' He's a fellow fan and he thinks this is the best thing he's ever seen in his life.

He then drags me by my collar and takes me out of the hotel to meet his family. His English isn't great, but he keeps tapping me on my head, and then his phone, and saying, 'It is him, it is him.' Wonderful. We take a few photos with his family and I am away up to my room.

Cologne, of course, is also full of many Swiss fans. Like the Scots they travel well, and being a bordering country, there are thousands of them. Now, it was a long time ago, but I have a bit of history with the Swiss, and my goal against them in the 1996 Euros in England, at Villa Park, remains one of my better strikes. The night before the game in Cologne, we are out having a few beers, and amongst us is a big group of Swiss fans.

One of them walks over, and again the phone has come out. Here we go, AC bloody DC again, but no, to my surprise it's 1996 and my goal from some thirty-five yards (no, really). He's showing it to his mates, and we have a good laugh and reminisce about it.

Talking of goals, Scott McTominay's effort early in the game against Switzerland is a great release. All these Scottish fans who have come to Germany, many of whom cannot get into the stadium, are desperate for a moment of glory and

Scott's goal is an instant offering of pure joy. The goal goes in, and the vast majority of Scots are thinking that it's back on. We're winning the Euros. It's sorted.

I have to keep my voice low, and not show too much in the way of emotion, but I am standing up and my fist is both clenched and hitting the air above me. It's magic. You can sense in the crowd, as they go ballistic, that a bit of belief and pride is restored. I feel that as a nation, sometimes all we want is an opportunity to celebrate, and that goal gives us that and more.

Of course, it doesn't last that long and the Swiss draw level soon after with a goal from Xherdan Shaqiri, which for me was right up there as goal of the tournament. It's a thing of beauty and so we're back to grafting, but we have a great go and the match might have gone either way.

It's a draw though, and whilst there is a slight disappointment to have gone ahead and not won, the draw means we're alive, the last game is not a dead rubber, and victory over the Hungarians will see us through. After the sheer horror of Munich, we are still in it, our destiny is in our own hands.

Another week of dreaming . . .

In 1990, having been dropped for that opening World Cup game against Costa Rica, I watched mostly from the bench (I got on for the last fifteen minutes), as we were beaten one-nothing. It wasn't a great start, we all knew the flak we'd get for letting such a minnow beat us, and we headed back to our base in Portofino with our tails between our legs.

The next game was against Sweden, and once again Andy Roxburgh and Craig Brown named the team in sections.

Once again, I am not playing. But, and this is the thing, neither is Alan McInally. The big man is fuming. Now it's time for *him* to march up the stairs, and he's on the phone to his old man, Jackie McInally, who once won the Scottish title with Kilmarnock. A wonderful guy, Jackie, and this is his turn to try and calm down his son.

I am walking along the corridor, and from our room I can hear big Al, effing and blinding on the phone. 'How can I be dropped? I was the only one to play okay against the Costa Ricans! Why has he taken it out on me?' All this stuff.

I walk into the room, Al politely says goodbye to his dad, and stares straight ahead, looking as if he is ready to fight the entire world. I should say something encouraging about knowing how he feels. Instead, I stand there and say, 'Hey, you.'

He turns slowly and looks at me. 'Wha d'you want?' he says.

I take my crossword book, fling it at him, and say, 'You'll be able to fucking help me with that tonight.'

As I say, sometimes you have to laugh . . .

six

THE GAFFERS

I T is ten minutes past midnight and that means I'm ten
minutes late. A disaster? Not if you're late for anyone else,
but I'm late for big Jock Wallace, and that means I'm in big
trouble. I'm standing alone outside our hotel, looking into
reception and wondering where my safest route lies. I take a
deep breath and I make my move. Maybe he won't notice.
Maybe things will be okay.

It is the summer of 1984. A pre-season tour to Switzerland
with Rangers, and we've been training and playing warm-up
fixtures, so on our last night the boss, Jock Wallace, tells the
lads that we can go out for a few local beers. But he wants us
all back, and this point is reinforced with the fierceness of
his eyes, by midnight.

To state that Jock was a hard man would earn anyone a
PhD in the art of understatement. A former miner, Jock was
also a soldier whose national service was gleefully served in

Northern Ireland and the Malay Peninsula, where he engaged in jungle warfare. Those of us who worked with him could only surmise that the jungle lost.

Jock Wallace, with his granite features, was a man with a growl that shook the bones of his players, and a desire for discipline within his ranks that never dropped below intense. So, when away with the team, us players knew that when the boss said he wanted us back by midnight, what he really meant was, see you at 11.59.

I am in the local pub, enjoying the last half of my pint, when I glance at my watch and it already reads 12.01. Gulp. I'm in trouble. I finish my drink (common sense suggests I should have left it, but common sense was lost earlier in the evening) and I head back to the hotel. It appears quiet.

News had reached us earlier that Jock was enjoying a few wee drams of his own that night in the hotel bar, so there is hope that he has had a few and has taken himself to bed. With that thought, I jog through reception, all clear, pass the hotel bar, all clear, head to the staircase, so far, so good . . . I might make it . . . but then, a toilet door opens and out walks Jock, straight into my path, and all hope is lost.

He looks me up and down. No need to check his watch, he knows I'm late, probably by the fear in my eyes. There is no screaming, no swearing, just the clenching of his jaw, and that growl that is followed by the words, 'You, get up those fuckin' stairs. I'll see you in a minute.'

I make my way up. I've been rooming with a new signing, Cammy Fraser. Cammy is in our room and smoking one of his wee Panatella cigars, oblivious to the hell coming my way.

That is until he sees me enter the room, with the fear of god in my eyes.

'Wha's wrong with you?'

'I'm in trouble, Cammy. Big trouble.'

'Why?'

'I missed the boss's midnight curfew. He's on his way up.'

'Ah, dinnae worry about all that, Coisty. He winnae be that angry with you.'

As I say, Cammy is a new signing, probably not versed in Jock Wallace's legendary temper.

'Cammy, I am aware that it is not your jaw that is goin' to get cracked, but I would be grateful if you would show me a little bit more concern here.'

He has another wee puff of his cigar. 'Listen, Coisty, when the gaffer gets up here, I'll sort it, man. I'll be at your side, I'll help calm him down.'

There is a knock at the door. Actually, it's more like a crack at the door, like an earthquake. It's Jock. Here we go. Cammy gets up from his bed and stubs his cigar into the ash tray. 'I'll sort this,' he says. He heads to the door, pauses, turns right, walks into the bathroom and locks the door. I'm on my own.

Another crack at the door. I have to open it, so I do, and Jock is straight in the room, a grimace across his face. Before I can argue my case, he's given me a punch, a short-ranged jab, a hard dink, but enough to rock me onto my heels and down onto my arse. I'm stunned, and as I open my eyes, Jock's face is in mine.

'You're late, and it ne'er happens again, are we understood?'

Jock leaves as quickly as he came in. The door slams shut, and I get up. The stunned silence is broken only by a wee knock from the toilet door and Cammy's voice. 'Is he away, yet?'

It's a story that the modern footballer could not comprehend. The idea of a curfew being necessary in today's game would baffle a player just as much as the notion that a manager could hit one of them. The thing is, when I think back on that story, the same thought enters my head that I had that night. *I deserved it.*

Back when I was playing, it was a manager's right to lose their rag with players, a right they enthusiastically and regularly enforced, and in Scotland, a manager was always seen as very much 'The Boss'. Many people might hold an image of the Scottish manager. He wears an old macintosh, has Brylcreemed hair, he's gruff, he's fierce, and he's always on the verge of a violent outburst. I'm not saying that image is not often an accurate one, but especially for my own generation, a Scottish manager came with an aura that demanded respect.

Your dad and your uncles were one thing, but it could be the schoolteacher, the bus driver or the fella in the post office, us kids knew to greet certain people with a degree of reverence and awe. From a young age, for those of us who played football, the coaches and managers were always held in the highest of esteem. That never changed. When you think of all the great things Scotland has given the world, football managers have to be up there with whisky and golf.

My first real brush with true eminence came in 1980, when I was selected to travel with Scotland's semi-professional squad for a tournament in Holland. I was seventeen, playing for St Johnstone. It was my first time abroad in a football capacity, and the excitement that came with that was only made greater when we discovered that Jock Stein, now the Scotland manager, had travelled over to join us.

I have never known a room's atmosphere change as much as it would when Jock entered its door. Even calling him Jock now seems wrong. It was always Mr Stein. We had some great young lads. Gerry McCabe, Jim Fallon from Clydebank, Gerry Christie, wee Jamie Fairley from Hamilton, big John Kennedy with St Johnstone, all making our way at some level of the game.

I didn't play in the tournament, but it was a great experience for a seventeen-year-old, and after we beat the English 2–0 in the final, the celebrations went long into the Amsterdam night. My fellow teammates might be reading this, so I won't divulge too much, but let's just say that as a mere teenager, I can't be sure that much of what I did that night was legal.

Jock Stein had this way about him, a knowing walk, a glance followed by words of wisdom. The management staff with us, led by Bill Munro, the manager, were noticeably affected by his arrival. It was never negative or overbearing, it was just that way he had, a combination of knowledge and gravitas that was unsurpassed. We were a bunch of semi- or young pros from the First Division, but his presence didn't half add a touch of glamour and it gave us all extra focus.

I was at the height of my punk obsession. The music I was listening to back home, and the gigs we all made sure we had tickets for, were very much about smashing the system. The establishment was there to be brought down and the soundtrack to it all was the Sex Pistols and The Clash. But when Mr Stein strolled into a room, any punk notions were put on the back burner. This was a man at the sharp end of Scottish (or even world) football's top table, and such anarchistic thoughts melted away. I would go so far as to say that one chat with the big man, and even a young John Lydon and Joe Strummer would have offered a bow. A meeting of minds that I would have given anything to witness.

Men such as Stein were hard but fair. I worked with three of the best. The big man, Sir Alex Ferguson and Walter Smith, all of them peas from the same pod. Solid, hardworking, honest, fair, no-nonsense types, with the highest of expectations when it came to standards. All had the ability to crack a joke, but you were never 100 per cent certain they were joking. They would leave you with a wisecrack, but with a lingering doubt, and you knew that they were enjoying your slight confusion. You can't teach that.

It wasn't just the great managers I worked with who put the fear of god into me. Even those no longer with us maintained that aura and the ability to make certain you knew of their presence. One that springs to mind is the great Bill Struth, the Rangers manager who won eighteen Scottish titles between 1920 and 1954.

Quite rightly, the Rangers' trophy room that he filled so regularly has long had his portrait on its walls, and I swear his eyes follow you around the room until you feel that he's breathing down your neck. I was manager at Ibrox, and his presence was both an inspiration and a reminder of the standards he set.

When it comes to Scotland's managerial standards, the benchmark remains three men. Jock Stein, Sir Matt Busby and Bill Shankly. Three names forged into the country's footballing Mount Rushmore. Three men from similar stock, who all experienced life at those dark coalfaces, and who lived those experiences and created football teams built on them. Like life underground, the sides at Celtic, Manchester United and Liverpool bristled with energy, hard work and never-ending camaraderie. They remain amongst the biggest and most well-supported clubs on the planet, and for that, all three can thank men from Lanarkshire and its Ayrshire borders.

I never had the pleasure of meeting Bill Shankly. However, such are the amount of anecdotes and quotes that come with the great man, I feel like I did. I love that Shanks was in Lisbon to watch Stein's Celtic win the European Cup and summed it up perfectly when he told the Celtic boss after their 2–1 win over Internazionale, 'John [never Jock], you're immortal now.' As ever, he wasn't wrong.

My favourite line of Shankly's tells you all you need to know about his unerring work ethic. 'When I go, I am going to be the fittest man ever to die.' What a line. When he left us in 1981, too young at only sixty-eight years old and seemingly still so full of life and verve, you have to suspect that he got his wish.

I did meet Sir Matt. It was the early 1990s and I was invited down to Manchester by the wonderful Gordon McQueen, who stayed in the next village from me and had become a close friend. Big Derek Johnstone joined us too. Gordon was ex-Manchester United and he asked if we would join him for some brunch at Norman Whiteside's house, followed by a trip to Old Trafford for a match, *and* the chance to meet the great man.

What Sir Matt achieved at Manchester United is hard to put into words. The trophies are one thing, the longevity another, but to have gone through what he did after the Munich air disaster in 1958, to have found the strength not only to step back into the role of manager, but to build another team good enough ten years later to win the European Cup; well, it transcends football and will never be forgotten. It has to be one of the greatest sports stories, no, the greatest stories of all time.

That day with Gordon and Derek, after a brunch at Norman's house (not your usual bacon and eggs, by the way), we got to the stadium and had the pleasure of being introduced. Gordon is a big man, played for the club and had met Sir Matt before but still, the respectful nervousness that we all felt as we went into the room to say hello was very clear. It was a healthy anticipation. Not that we needed to be nervous. Sir Matt was the most gently spoken man, with a wonderful way of making you feel special. I could see why his players loved him.

What he did, like so many of these great managers, was show an incredible interest in you as an individual. I was playing at Rangers, and he asked me questions about my life, how I was playing, if I was enjoying my football. He had such knowledge about us all, and about the game up in his home country. He was amongst the most genuine men I have ever met. All three of us left him feeling ten feet tall.

I can't say I felt as confident about myself and my position after one of my early meetings with Stein. It was my first call-up into his Scotland squad. We were trying to qualify for the 1986 World Cup in Mexico, and having done well with Rangers, I was excited to be around some great players and, of course, work with the great Jock Stein.

I was young, early twenties, and very keen to impress. 'Yes, Mr Stein' and 'Thank you, Mr Stein.' I was also with these big players and on occasion at Gleneagles, after training, I would sit in the cafeteria with Kenny Dalglish, Steve Nicol and Alan Hansen.

We are talking one day and Kenny gets up. 'Right, what do you want to drink?'

Jockey Hansen orders a black coffee, Stevie asks for a tea, and I ask for a coffee, too. As Kenny moves over to get the drinks, Stein walks into the room, and sits down with us for a blether. 'How is everything, Ally?'

'Perfect, thank you, Mr Stein.'

'Enjoying the training?'

'Aye, Mr Stein. It's magic.'

As we're talking, Kenny comes back with the drinks. He puts the black coffee in front of Jockey, the tea in front of Stevie Nicol, and in front of me, a full pint of lager.

'There you go, Coisty,' he says with a straight face. 'There's the pint you were after.'

Oh my god. I'm trying to splutter out some words, trying to convince the great Jock Stein that this is not what I ordered, and that I am a model pro. 'But . . . No . . . That's not, what . . .'

Before I can get a coherent sentence from my stunned mouth, the manager has got up and is walking out. Kenny, Jockey and Stevie can no longer contain their laughter, and

I'm left with a face the colour of beetroot, and the fear that one of the greatest men ever to pick a football team thinks his young centre forward is a piss-head.

Part of me thinks Jock was in on the joke, judging by his under-reaction, the fact that he picked me in his next squad, and the ever-so-wry grin he gave as he got up and left. But such was the level of sheer awe I had for him, some forty years later, I am still riddled with fear, hoping beyond hope that the great man didn't think ill of me. Thanks, Kenny! Even telling the story now, I can feel the intense terror I felt when that bastard placed the pint in front of me and Mr Stein.

The thing that these three managers, Stein, Busby and Shankly, have in common, as well as sheer achievement, is legacy. Not just in the gargantuan size of their clubs (all of which were in bad shape before they joined), but the men who worked under them in some capacity and went on to achieve so much. If Johan Cruyff is lauded for producing Pep Guardiola, then Stein, Busby and Shankly can all take some credit for a long line of Scottish managers that includes Sir Alex Ferguson, Kenny Dalglish, Graeme Souness, Gordon Strachan, Walter Smith, Billy McNeil, and many others. They all spawned from the great three. That would have made them as happy as anything they won.

Of those names, Sir Alex Ferguson obviously stands out. Arguably Britain's greatest manager of all time, my first experiences of the man were on those memorable trips from my home in East Kilbride as a teenager with him and the young Stevie Cowan to train at St Mirren, before eventually being told that I would not be getting signed by the club. It was a horrible moment.

Having been a manager myself, I can say that the very worst part of the job – never mind the losing, or the pressure from the crowd – was telling young players that you weren't taking them on. Sir Alex had looked me in the eye and said, 'Son, I am so sorry, but I feel that at this moment you are just too small.'

Words that stung, but Sir Alex talked to me in a way that gave me hope. 'Look, Ally, don't be too down. I know it isn't what you want to hear but you go home, get out there, work hard and you prove me wrong. And by the way, there won't be anyone happier than me if that's exactly what you do.' That had an effect on me, and I always tried to say the same things to kids that I had to let go.

I did soon get to prove him wrong, but even as a professional back at Rangers, Sir Alex was able to break my own and most 'Gers fans' hearts with his Aberdeen side, who created a 'New Firm', along with Jim McLean's Dundee United, that would often beat Celtic and Rangers and won plenty of the silverware on offer. Sir Alex's Aberdeen were especially brilliant. There was a spell when we went to Pittodrie and getting heavily beaten was far from unusual. They were very much the real deal, in those early and mid-1980s days, and with their manager, there were never, ever going to be signs of an inferiority complex.

I was very pally with a lot of the Aberdeen boys, having played youth football with them. Eric Black and I even went to the same primary school together. A fantastic player. The side was full of them. McLeish, Miller, Strachan, McGhee,

McMaster, Rougvie, Kennedy; I could go on. It was some team, but don't be fooled. Yes, they may have taken on and beaten up the Old Firm, and yes, they were massive characters, but Sir Alex could still put the fear of god up them.

Neale Cooper, Johnny Hewitt and Andy Dornan were great pals of mine. I would go up there and visit, and they would have me in stitches about their gaffer. Fergie used to go mental at them on a regular basis and it was all about trying to get away with things. They had a weights room, an exercise room for rehab, but in it there was also a pool table. Fergie hated that pool table, especially when injured players who should be pushing some weights were messing about on it. To be caught playing pool instead of doing your exercises was punishable with death.

Fergie also had this cough. He and his assistant Archie Knox would prowl the corridors, but often the cough gave them away, giving his players a bit of valuable time to stop whatever it was they were doing, in this case playing pool.

On one occasion though, Fergie came down the stairs, but there was no cough. He marched into the room and the boys were playing pool. Neale Cooper was leaning over the table, about to play his shot, when he looked up, saw his gaffer about to go into a DEFCON 1 level of rage, and without flinching, he put the pool cue above his head and started doing squats. Later, the boys asked, 'What the hell did you do that for?'

To which the late, great Neale replied, 'I don't know, I was just that scared!'

I made my own way into the pro game at St Johnstone, having been signed by Alex Stuart. I wasn't a full-time pro, but it was the best education working with great football men like Stuart, and it was a successor of his, Alex Rennie, who changed my career by suggesting I was better suited at centre forward. I had been playing in midfield, and Alex Stuart liked me seeing things and breaking into the box from deeper positions, but when Rennie got the job, he saw it differently and stuck me up front with big John Brogan.

That's the thing about Scottish managers, as well as the huge presence that so many of them possess, they have an eye for the game and can tweak aspects of a match or a player's game in positive ways. I owe Alex Rennie a lot, a wonderful man.

As I do John Greig, the Rangers legend who signed me from Sunderland. John was my hero as a boy, and I felt for Greigy, in the respect that he took over at Ibrox at a time when the team needed substantial changing. Jock Wallace had left after his first successful spell at the club and John was unlucky, partly because Sir Alex and Jim McLean, without any financial disparity, were building their two clubs' best ever sides. Greigy was rightly voted 'The Greatest Ever Ranger', and he was. I owe him everything for getting me to the club. I knew him as a player, my hero, and I knew him as a manager there, and he did everything for the club.

He managed softly, unlike the way he played, and perhaps he saw the game changing, becoming more modern. When he left, with the 'New Firm' blossoming, even Jock Wallace's return was no guarantee of success. For all of big Jock's ferocity, he was a very caring and even lovable man. He had won plenty of honours in his first spell and a couple of League

Cups in that second, but even he couldn't turn back the tide coming in from Aberdeenshire and Dundee.

What Rangers needed was Graeme Souness, and when the then 33-year-old Edinburgh man joined the club as player-manager in 1986, he set about creating what I regard as the biggest shake-up that Scottish (or possibly British) football has ever seen. Souness was a winner, we knew that from his playing days, a Rolls-Royce footballer but with a fondness for demolition derbies.

As soon as Graeme came in through the old doors at Ibrox, the swagger was there, and he basically said, right, I am driving this bus, if you want to get on, get on, but I am warning you now there will be sharp turns, there will be big bumps, and there will be fun. We were sold straight away and all jumped aboard.

His first three signings that summer were Colin West, Chris Woods and Terry Butcher: an English striker, the England goalkeeper and the England captain. And it didn't end there. It was unprecedented. The eyes of the world were suddenly on us and Scottish football.

Souness loved attention and he relished taking flak from supporters or the press or whoever; he would take it so his players didn't need to. Look at the signing of Mo Johnston, a former Celtic hero, from Nantes in 1989. To say the move on both Mo's and Graeme's part was 'ballsy' doesn't do it justice. Only Mo can answer the question, but I doubt he would have made that move for any other manager. Who else could have taken on the chin all the hostility that came with the move, absorbed all the grief, and let Mo get on with playing. And could he play, by the way?

The whole thing under Souness was all action. Ibrox was jumping, training was electric, results brilliant and the trophies rolled in. One stand-out occasion was the 5–1 win over Celtic in August 1988.

We are playing great that day, but with about ten minutes left, Graeme brings himself on. We are 5–1 up, but still relishing the energy of the game. Graeme comes on but the lads have had a word with each other. Don't pass to him. 'He'll only want to put his foot on the ball, and slow things down,' was one shout. We wanted more goals!

So, he gets on, he's making himself available, doing all the right things, and for about two minutes, he's not getting a pass. Hilarious. After a while, he twigs, and I can still see the smile come across his face. 'These bastards are doing me, here.' He found the funny side. Eventually.

Not that it was always so easy to coax a smile from under that moustache. Soon after Graeme came in, we used to play five-a-sides in training. England vs Scotland. Their team looked like a who's-who of the game, south of the border. Woods in goal, Butcher, Graham Roberts, Ray Wilkins, Trevor Francis, the depth was incredible. The thing is, Souness always used to play for them, and that drove us Scots insane with rage, which is exactly why he did it.

One Friday, the game gets going and as ever, it's full on. We are fired up. Myself, Davie Cooper, Ian Durrant, Nicky Walker in goal, Stuart Munro; we're well up for it and we are battering them. We're turning it on, back-heels, flicks, nutmegs, one-twos, the works, and we're soon 4–1 up.

Graeme is not happy. Raging. I can see his tolerance levels dropping rapidly when Durranty, the main conductor in our team's glorious concerto, receives the ball, and from his right, the manager storms in, and crack, he cements him. Bang! It's a very solid challenge, but instead of going over, Durranty does this Weeble Wobble thing. He kind of falls to one side but somehow bounces back, and is standing in front of his manager and assaulter. He puts his foot on the ball, looks Graeme in the eye and says, 'Is that your fuckin' best?'

Silence. Us Scots trying not to laugh, the English wondering about the brass balls on their young teammate. Graeme walks closer and says, 'No, this is,' and he puts a punch on Durranty that this time he doesn't bounce back from. Mayhem. It's all in, a bar-brawl from a Western movie, and there's punches, knees, kicks and head-butts everywhere.

I'm trying to throw counter-punches at Graeme, Butcher has me in a headlock, and Coops is getting volleyed by Roberts. All the while, Graeme's assistant, Walter Smith, is frantically blowing his whistle with the optimistic hope that it might end the madness. It doesn't and all you can hear is Walter's voice rising above the sounds of violence. 'You're a disgrace, you're all a fuckin' disgrace!'

The whole thing is going on at the Albion, the training ground we sometimes used near Ibrox. When the fighting eventually dies down, we walk back to the stadium, still in our groups. Us Scots on one pavement, the English and Souness on the other.

'You bunch of pricks!'

'You're totally out of order!'

We must have looked like rival schoolboys rather than adult athletes, and when we all get into the dressing room at

Ibrox, the Queen's portrait sits above us and I swear she has a disapproving look on her face.

We wait for Graeme to walk in. I have an icepack on my eye, Durranty has a golf-ball growing from his cheek, and we're all giving each other evil stares. We're left wondering what kind of bollocking the manager will give us – despite him starting the whole thing. Then he marches in, stands in the middle of the room, takes a breath, and says, 'That is exactly the kind of spirit I am looking for!'

The following day we got beat one-nothing by Dundee United at Ibrox.

The man with the whistle that day, Walter Smith, went on to succeed Graeme when he left for Liverpool in 1991 and continued the success, taking us very close to Champions League glory, and equalling Celtic's record of nine titles in a row. We could go on about Walter's achievements in the game, not many won more, but to me Walter was everything. A coach, an assistant manager always available to the players, a manager, but mainly a friend. He was without a doubt the greatest influence on my career and arguably my whole life.

At international level, I worked mainly under Andy Roxburgh and Craig Brown. Two students of the game. They didn't have that – it's hard to find the right word – but the same presence as some of the big men I have mentioned. I don't mean that negatively in any way, but they were products of a new era, fully focused on the intricacies of the game, without relying on the strength of personality. They had come from different environments to a Jock Stein or a Sir Alex Ferguson, and rather than trying to be someone they weren't, they managed their way, and everything was looked at in the most minute detail.

The game had become very different, far more technical. Stats and data were beginning to come into it, and every little detail was covered. The more old-school managers might not have been too interested in such things, but Andy and Craig were almost ahead of their times. Andy would go on to work with UEFA on technical matters, and Craig was greatly respected. It's no wonder. Working together, they got Scotland to the 1990 World Cup, the 1992 European Championships, and then under Craig, qualification was gained to the 1996 Euros and the 1998 World Cup.

World Cups, European Championships, Scottish titles and success in England is all well and good, and I loved working with the many greats who did that, but I also need to mention a manager who gave me some of, if not perhaps my most happiest times. Bobby Williamson was an ex-teammate of mine at Rangers, and in 1998, he convinced me and Durranty to join his Kilmarnock side. We had the best time, the dressing room was magic, and I'd like to think that the two of us brought some real drive and determination to an already fantastic squad.

We had great characters. Wee Mark 'Mavis' Reilly, Kevin McGowne, Martin Baker, Gus MacPherson, wee Ally Mitchell, or 'Bully'. The wee man was from Fife and I swear, people think Glaswegian is hard to understand, but I had to send his sentences to Bletchley Park to decipher.

It was a joy to be with so many great lads, some ex-Celtic, us ex-Rangers, and going into work was a pleasure. Every day. Neither Durranty or myself, however, were there to see out our careers leisurely. Sure, there were a lot of smiles and laughter along the way, but we gave everything to Bobby's team, and if anyone saw us training, they would say just how fully engaged we all were.

Arguably the most distraught I have ever been on a football pitch was at Rugby Park, when we got knocked out of the cup by Hibernian. I can see it now, a last-minute, back-post header. I was raging. Gutted. I remember it like it was yesterday. We could have gone on to win the cup that year!

Bobby himself was magnificent. He was of the old school (his pre-seasons were not for the faint-hearted), but he was also taking to the modernity of the job, and incredibly, having won the Scottish Cup in 1997, he took Kilmarnock to Europe for three consecutive seasons. That's truly remarkable. We were getting 14,000 crowds, which is incredible too, and they were the perfect days to end my own career.

Management is about being yourself, but when I had a stint as a boss, it would have been criminal of me not to have drawn on the experiences and the many characteristics of these global greats that I had the pleasure of working under. I had my own ideas, but how could I not learn from the schooling I was fortunate to have had?

These guys, Stein, Sir Alex, Walter, Souness, all of the managers I played under brought so much to the game and to Scotland. Their achievements and the honours they all won is alone something to gasp at, but I think I am even more impressed with the men they were. Each of them displayed great Scottish traits. Not the kind we see on battlefields in movies like *Braveheart*, but everyday attributes. They had a rawness, a realness, a fairness, a hardness, and plenty of humour to them, which made them not only the best, but wonderful to work with.

I love thinking about them all. I love reminiscing about them, laughing about them, and remembering the great times they all gave me. I am very lucky. I am fortunate to have worked with some of the best managers Scotland has ever produced and now, looking back on my own career playing the game, I can be nothing but proud to say that I was touched – or in the case of big Jock Wallace, punched – by genius.

seven

ON THE ROAD

The hairline retreats, the knee gets creakier, and bizarrely the waist on my trousers gets smaller with each wash. Looking in the mirror is like being introduced to a stranger, and the children I have brought up refuse to believe that the old man in the house who makes strange noises each time he sits down or gets up from the sofa, was once the top goalscorer in European football.

Growing old might come with sighs, but with all that, the showreel of memories that remain in my head can instantly take me to wonderful times, with the best of people and to faraway places. They remind me that through a bit of hard work, a tiny bit of talent and a sprinkling of fortune, I was able to play at the highest level of the game, with and against some of the biggest names in the modern era, whilst having the absolute time of my life.

Between 1987 and 1993, I believe I was playing not only my best football, but my club side became the best in Britain, and the international side remained able to compete in major tournaments against the best in Europe and the world. With hindsight, and like the ageing process itself, Scotland's inability to progress past the group stages did come with a painful inevitability, but nonetheless, we were throwing good punches and some even landed.

One of the great bouts was in a World Cup qualifying match against France. It was March 1989, and whilst the French were no longer the vintage of Jean Tigana and Michel Platini (he was there as the coach), and some way off from maturing into their full-bodied 1998 winning team, they were still very good. We faced plenty of great talent that night and to win at Hampden, we needed to be our very best. We were, but so was the weather. As the Glaswegian rain blew horizontally – or 'steadily' as the legendary commentator and king of the understatement, Archie Macpherson, put it on the night – we flew into our guests.

Our good start was strange, because we had driven down from our camp at Gleneagles and got caught in terrible traffic, compounded by the rain, and didn't get to the stadium until about half an hour before kick-off. It was probably the first (and last) time Andy Roxburgh was late for anything. They hadn't delayed the match, so it was a case of get in, get changed and get out there. Maybe all the modern warm-ups are a waste of time, because we were rocking from the off.

Mo Johnston and I were playing up front. We had been playing well with each other for Scotland, and in a few months we'd be brought together at club level too. Wee Mo was a joy to play with. He was nippy and loved to get in behind, and although we were never what was deemed to be a perfect pairing on paper, our similarities worked. We knew what the other would do, second-guessed defenders in unison, and Mo being constantly on the front foot allowed me to drop into some deeper pockets of space.

Against France, even with defenders of the calibre of Manuel Amoros, Laurent Blanc and Patrick Battiston, we got very much amongst them. Mo gave us the lead, before doubling the advantage in the second half. I scored a third, a cracker into the top corner, but Mo was ruled offside. He was nowhere near me or interfering with play, and the goal would be given nowadays.

I think of it every time I see Mo, and I remind him of his lackadaisical positioning, and if you're wondering, no, I am not over it, and at times I still count it in my goal tally: *Ally McCoist, 19 goals for Scotland. *It should have been 20!*

Despite my grievances, it was right up there with one of the finest international displays that I was involved in, especially so given the opposition and the stakes. We were well on our way, and despite a couple of defeats at the end of the qualifying stages, my goal against Norway ensured us a summer in Italy.

The location of the 1990 World Cup only added to the sense of excitement. As we entered the new decade, Italy was firmly at the epicentre of world football. Serie A had the very best players, with stars such as Diego Maradona and Lothar Matthäus amongst the many jewels in its crown. It housed one of the best teams, namely AC Milan, who with Frank Rijkaard, Ruud Gullit and Marco van Basten were playing football from another planet. They also had the public, and with the World Cup on its way, they would soon have the stadia.

The draw set us against the Swedes, Brazil and the unknown Costa Rica. We would play our games in the north-west of the country, Turin and Genoa, and our base was the strangely named Hotel Bristol in the town of Rapallo on the Italian riviera. Now, no offence to the good people of Bristol, but the absolute luxury and picturesque coastal setting of our Italian base bore little resemblance to Temple Meads or Ashton Gate!

As the players walked into the place, the blue Ligurian Sea shimmering at our backs, to a man, we audibly thanked those clever blokes at the Scottish FA. It's a rarity for the men in suits to enjoy such acclaim from any squad, but such was the beauty of the location, it was richly warranted on this occasion. They might also be feeling good about themselves regarding the appointment of Andy Roxburgh as Scotland manager, a man who had long worked within the walls of the SFA, a former schoolteacher, but one who had now led us to this special place.

At his side was Craig Brown and, whilst dissimilar in character, both men looked at football in the same way, which was quite different to either Jock Stein or Alex Ferguson. Like his predecessors, Andy demanded discipline, punctuality and respect, and he got all three, but you noticed he was that bit more methodical. He looked at the smallest details, demanding that no one wore strapping on their socks. We also had to wear the same T-shirts under our tracksuits, and tracksuits had to be worn at all times. Basically all very uniform. Sometimes it seemed too much like micromanaging, but we all liked Andy, and so got on with it.

Under his stewardship, since the previous World Cup in Mexico, the make-up of the squad had changed considerably.

Jim Leighton, Paul McStay and Roy Aitken gave us some tournament experience, but they were joined by an eager bunch of new players, chomping at the bit to have a go at progressing through the group stages.

We had done well to qualify, beating the French and competing with the Yugoslavs, who would enjoy an impressive competition. However, we had lost a few warm-up games, including a 3–1 defeat to Egypt at Pittodrie, a result that invited some stick from the press and some doubters amongst the public. Only weeks earlier, the lads had beaten the world champions, Argentina, one-nothing at Hampden, so whilst the press and public scoffed at us, we simply took the Egypt result as a wake-up call.

I arrived in Italy hopeful of starting up front with Mo Johnston. By now, the wee man had made his much talked about move to Rangers, and together we had found the net with title-winning regularity. The move had antagonised a lot of people, but with Graeme Souness caring very little for such matters, Mo was left to get on with it. Well, kind of.

It was a tense situation and I knew what was happening before most people. I had been away with Scotland with Mo, who was with Nantes in France at the time. Mo would chat to me and on occasion he would mention things about the inside of Souness's house. I was thinking, how the hell does the wee man know about Graeme's interiors? He gave me that wee grin of his and I was sworn to secrecy.

I knew it would be a fiery signature, but none of us could have predicted that Mo's signing would make Glasgow stand still. It even brought some Rangers and Celtic fans together in rage. Some Celtic fans were furious with Mo and some

Rangers fans were furious with their club. Shirts, scarves and season tickets were being burnt, but we had someone able to take the sting out of such situations. Our magic kit man at Rangers, Jimmy Bell. What a character he was.

The summer Mo signed, we went off to our training camp at Il Ciocco, in Tuscany. Jimmy used to lay out all the kit individually outside everyone's hotel room and on top of each meticulous pile of gear, he'd leave us all a nice bar of chocolate. Well, on our first day in Italy, Mo came out of his room, and there was nothing. He had to go and get his own gear. Mo was fuming, but as we headed to training, Jimmy shouted, 'Tell tha' wee bastar' tha he'll get his gear folded and some chocolate once he scores against the Celtic!'

It brought the house down, Mo was in hysterics, it relaxed the mood around the place, and Mo and Jimmy became the best of pals. The wee man couldn't find the net in the first August Old Firm clash, but his sweet tooth was satiated after a last-minute winner at Ibrox in November, and by the way, such was the celebratory nature of his goal, I think he got two bars of chocolate.

Mo Johnston was brilliant, absolutely magnificent with me at Rangers and for the national team. In fact, I would go so far as to say that in that period in and around the 1990 World Cup, he was right up there with the best strikers in the world. With that form, it was always going to be about who played up top with him. I would never presume to play for Scotland, but I was hopeful, given the partnership we had formed at Rangers and how easily we had continued that form at international level.

The Wembley Wizards! The game might have been won way back in 1928, but the team that went to Wembley and beat England 5–1 will always have a place in Scottish hearts.

We're the kings of the world! The brilliant Jim Baxter gets a hug for helping Scotland beat the then World Champions, England, at Wembley in 1967.

I was devastated not to be picked in the squad for the 1998 World Cup, but that was never going to stop me backing the boys. Here I am in my Rangers tartan, leaving the stadium in Bordeaux after our 1–1 draw with Norway.

We're all off to Italy! Testing the Norway defence in a game that saw my goal help the team get to the 1990 World Cup.

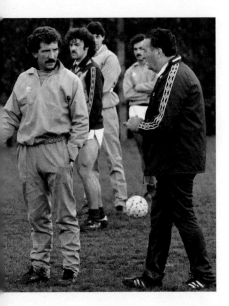

Giants! The big man, Jock Stein, passes his knowledge on to Graeme Souness. Judging by John Wark and Willie Miller behind them, moustaches were all the rage.

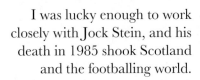

I was lucky enough to work closely with Jock Stein, and his death in 1985 shook Scotland and the footballing world.

The wee man in a big hat! Gordon Strachan was one of many brilliant players in the 1982 World Cup squad.

World Class! Two of our greatest players, Kenny Dalglish and Danny McGrain are all smiles having helped us win the 1976 Home Championships.

A rare moment of calm contemplation with my friend and club teammate, Paul Gascoigne. What a player and what a goal he's just scored against us in the summer of 1996.

Suited and booted! Myself, Scott Booth, Pat Nevin and Eoin Jess are the four goal scorers in a 5–1 win against San Marino in 1995.

Shoulda scored! Peter Shilton (in a Scottish goalkeeper shirt) thwarts my effort in the Rous Cup game at Hampden in 1989.

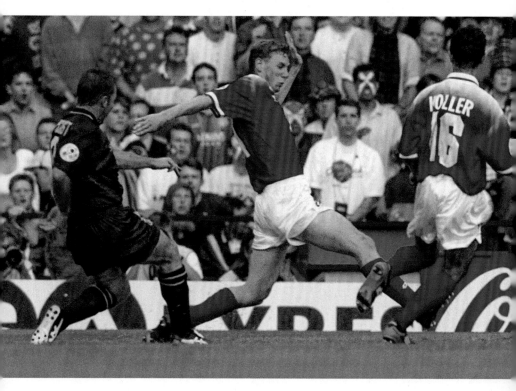

Making the Swiss roll! I couldn't have hit my effort in the 1996 Euros any sweeter . . . unfortunately it wasn't enough.

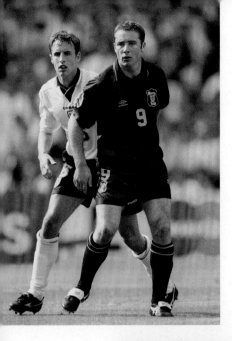

It wasn't to be. Gareth Southgate keeps a keen eye on me during our loss to England in 1996.

I'd grown up watching Brazil and it was a pleasure to play against them at Hampden in 1987. *They were lucky to win 2–0.

Walter Smith asked myself and the great Tommy Burns to assist him with the national team in 2004. It was both the best fun and the greatest honour of my life . . .

The greatest fans in the world! The Tartan Army never fail to make me proud.

No Scotland, No Party! Scotland fans merrily arrive in
Germany for the 1974 World Cup.

Of the five strikers who travelled to Mexico in 1986, none had remained in the national squad. I remember one game in 1987. We were playing Belgium, and myself and Paul Sturrock, or Luggy as I call him, were up front. Luggy had gone to the 1982 and 1986 World Cups and was always a pleasure to play alongside. Such a clever footballer.

Not on this occasion though. We were getting thrashed. The Belgians scored their fourth in a 4–1 win, and as we waited for the ball to return slowly to the centre circle, Luggy turned to me, let out a sigh, took in the surroundings and the crowd and said solemnly, 'Ach well, Coisty. Here endeth an illustrious international career.'

It was such a great line, so great, I had to suppress a laugh right there in the centre circle. Luggy might well have been talking about both our careers, but whilst he never played for Scotland again, I was fortunate enough to get another chance, joining a new set of World Cup strikers, including Mo, Gordon Durie, Robert Fleck and my roommate, Alan McInally.

It was a strong set of forwards, but I'd be lying if I said I didn't fancy my chances of starting the first game against Costa Rica. I'd had a wee hamstring injury at the end of the season, but it had cleared up and was certainly not a factor in the decision that saw my hopes dashed by Andy Roxburgh. My subsequent temper tantrum was only dampened by the hilarity of my roommate McInally and that request for me to turn off the lights, as 'some of us have a game tomorrow'.

Rooming with Big Jake, as he was known due to his dad, the former Kilmarnock player Jackie McInally, was painfully funny. It was far from relaxing, due to the constant belly laughs, but pleasurable nonetheless. On arriving in Italy, the squad gathered at an accreditation office to collect our passes. The room was aligned with some lights along its floor. For weeks, Andy had got us doing exercises that saw him lay out small cones. Coincidentally, these floor lights were spaced out in exactly the same way as Andy's cones, and whilst we were all waiting and getting bored, we turned and Big Jake was running from light to light, doing heel-taps and side-scissors. It was magic and the whole place was on the floor.

When we first walked up to our hotel room, the big man had me in further hysterics when he went into his bag, pulled out a colour poster of him in his Bayern Munich kit, and stuck it purposefully to the door.

'Wha' ya doin', big man?' I asked.

'I want everybody in this hotel to know where Big Jake from the München is stayin'!'

Like Alan, the whole squad was a joy to be around. I was very lucky with national team squads, as I never experienced a fractious one. There could be many reasons for Scottish groups to have problems. In the past, there was talk of the Anglophiles amongst World Cup squads forming cliques, and those who played their club football in England being somehow separated from the homegrown lads. It certainly wasn't an issue when I played.

What about us Old Firm lads? A school of thought suggested that there must be a 'them and us' situation within our squads, and with the intense rivalry, a closeness between Rangers and Celtic players could not possibly exist. Nothing could be further from the truth. I never witnessed or experienced any kind of issue with any of the Celtic lads and always counted men like Paul McStay and Roy Aitken as not just good teammates, but great pals.

Recently, a photo went around a WhatsApp group. Derek Whyte, the former Celtic, Aberdeen and Partick Thistle defender, had come across a photo of myself and Roy Aitken during an Old Firm clash in the mid-1980s. Unusually, I am wearing a number seven shirt, instead of the number nine, and Derek sent the photo, wondering why I was wearing the different number. I replied that seven was the number of times I went by big Roy in the first half alone.

Roy saw the message and had another version of events. 'Tell Ally he's talking a load of shite,' he said. 'Seven is actually the row I kicked him into in the second-half.'

Costa Rica were widely regarded as amongst the weakest teams in the 1990 World Cup. It was said that they were only there because Mexico had been banned from qualifying by FIFA due to playing overage players at an Under-20 tournament. Whatever their reasons for being there, for us Scots (with hindsight, worryingly), they represented the best chance of qualifying from the group stages.

A new format meant that a number of sides finishing in third place would progress to the knock-out stages, and so one win might be enough to see us go where no Scot had been before. The nation were certainly gearing up for the possibility. Costa Rica had lost to Wales in a warm-up fixture, and the *Scotsman* newspaper ran the headline: 'WARNING: COSTA RICA BEATABLE!'

In the camp, prior to the opening game, there was no complacency. How could there be? Our tournament

forefathers had fallen foul to Iran in 1978, a team described
by Ally MacLeod as 'minnows'. Andy's personality was chalk
to Ally's strong and mature cheese, and there would be no
such bravado. Instead we were well-schooled on the side's
strengths and weaknesses, and it was the latter that seemed
to get in the way of my hopes to start the game.

There was a suggestion that the Costa Rica manager, a
shrewd Serbian called Velibor Milutinović, had publicly said
that he feared McInally and that's why Big Jake got the nod.
It was also said that the Costa Rican keeper, Luis Gabelo
Conejo, was more than susceptible to crosses and so the big
man's considerable ability in the air would be an advantage.

As it turned out, Señor Gabelo Conejo was susceptible to
very little. Instead he had an absolute blinder, making save
after save, and clutching in-swingers for fun. From the subs
bench in the impressive Stadio Luigi Ferraris in Genoa, the
Italian afternoon heat was made more uncomfortable by the
Costa Ricans taking a second-half lead, and whilst I was happy
to get on and make my World Cup debut towards the end of
the game, our performance was nervy and unconvincing.

It was a chastening start and with some factions of the
Tartan Army singing 'What a load of rubbish!' into the
Genovese afternoon air, we returned to the hotel knowing
that the press were going to slaughter us. We were right. The
Scotsman called it the nation's poorest World Cup result ever.
Ouch.

That night, back at the hotel, Andy came to me. 'Ally,' he
said, 'your wee pal is down in the town and he's drinking champagne.' I knew immediately that he meant Mo. I had been
rooming with the wee man for a season at Rangers, and knew

from experience that he liked a drop of the bubbly stuff. One New Year's Eve, we were staying in a hotel. We were playing Celtic on 2nd January. After dinner, we were both in our room when wee Mo produced a bottle of the good stuff, Bollinger, and said, 'This is for you and I to bring in the bells, Alistair.'

'That'll do lovely, wee man,' I said with a smile. 'But just in case someone comes in, let's hide it behind the curtains.'

Mo did, and then at about 11.30, the door opened and it was the assistant manager, Walter Smith.

'How are you lads?' he asked.

'Yes, very good, Walter.'

'Looking forward to the game?'

'Canae wait, Walter.'

He walked right over to the curtains, drew them, and said, 'Looks like I'm gonna have a fuckin' good New Year's.'

To this day I have no idea how he knew we had a bottle of Bollinger behind those curtains, but that's what Walter did, he knew everything.

Anyway, he left with wee Mo's bottle of Bollinger, thanked us very much and bid us farewell. About twenty-five minutes later, the door opened again and in walked Walter with a tray, the bottle of Bollinger on ice and three glasses, and we saw in the New Year together. Magic.

So, that night in Italy, the minute I heard champagne being mentioned, I knew the culprit was Mo. What surprised me was that he had taken Jim Bett along with him. Jimmy Bett has probably not had a glass of beer in his life, let alone champagne. He was the most unlikely of accomplices, but word had made its way back to the manager that both were indulging.

'Your pal is in the town drinking champagne, and I want you to go and get him.'

'Andy,' I said. 'There is absolutely no danger of me going into Rapallo and telling Mo to stop drinking his champagne and to come back with me. If he won't listen to you, there is no chance that he will listen to me.' Not long after, the two of them strolled back into the hotel. It was rather obvious that a couple of bottles had been taken, and a bollocking was handed out by Andy and Craig.

After the defeat, those lads who hadn't taken to the champers were clearly very down. Andy tried to remain positive, using stats (a new fad in the game whose longevity we questioned) to prove all was not lost. He could argue with the press that we'd had nineteen shots to Costa Rica's four, but we all knew that the level of performance in the second game against Sweden would have to be significantly higher.

It is hard being a squad player, with your own grievances about not playing, whilst still wanting to be upbeat, especially after a bad defeat. The lads who started were down because of the loss, I was down because of the loss *and* not playing in it. It was one of the biggest disappointments in my career, not starting that game.

I didn't kick off with Andy, as that wouldn't be fair. I pulled him to one side and asked about his decision; he gave me his explanation, I didn't agree with it and we moved on. That's how it works. I felt let down though. I'd scored a couple of goals in the qualifying stages and contributed well, but that's football. It was a strange situation. I had no right to feel let down, but that was the emotion. Later, I went into management, and I could draw on that feeling when it came time to leave people out.

However I felt, I tried to force a smile and as the days passed, you sensed that the defeat was behind us. The downtime at the Hotel Bristol was good. We were living in the most beautiful setting and boredom was never an issue. Table tennis and pool tables, plus Brian Henry, a terrific lad from Aberdeen, who could seemingly get most films anyone wanted. Card schools were always going, and we'd have all the other World Cup matches to take a look at as well.

The team selection for the Sweden game – once again done with Andy and Craig informing the players, position by position – brought more bad news, to me *and* Big Jake. Both of us were left to stew in our room after being dropped, a mood further darkened by the fact that both Gordon Durie and Norwich's Robert Fleck, a latecomer to the squad after Davie Cooper's unfortunate injury, had been picked to play up top with Mo. Flecky would be used in a wide position, where it was thought his pace could trouble their defence.

Gordon 'Jukebox' Durie was playing great stuff at Chelsea and Flecky had been with me at Rangers for a few seasons. Both were terrific strikers, fast and willing. Both were great lads too, but footballers are footballers and behind the closed door of our hotel room, Big Jake and I verbalised our individual reasons for believing that we should have been picked ahead of them both.

In the end though, Andy was vindicated and our 2–1 win, in a frantic game in Genoa, was just what the squad needed after Costa Rica. Stuart McCall, another new face in the group, was brilliant, scoring a goal and getting into the faces of the Swedes.

The Tartan Army were now singing our praises and whilst I didn't feel fully part of the win, it was great to know that should we draw with Brazil, we would go through. Easy, eh? They may not have been the Brazil of '82, but this was a Brazilian team housing Careca up front, a recent Serie A winner with Maradona's Napoli. The big man was partnered with a new prospect named Romario, whilst the likes of Taffarel in goal and Dunga in midfield offered established quality.

This time, the team selection 'meeting' brought me good news. I was in, up front with Mo. If the game against Sweden had been physical and played at a frantic tempo, the game in Turin was more considered. The Brazilians saw much of the ball, whilst we looked to be organised and compact, hoping to get Mo and myself involved further forward.

The weather was a possible help. It absolutely chucked it down that night in northern Italy. Definitely more Hebrides than Copacabana. The Tartan Army's bagpipes took on the samba drums of the Brazilian hordes, cheering us on, and an organised performance in the first half was only clouded by Murdo MacLeod's concussion.

Murdo was a great pal of mine and a fine player. Andy, being meticulous as ever, had worked on defensive walls in training (not a bad idea when facing the Brazilians), but on an occasion towards the end of the first half, we were slow to build it, and we set it up incorrectly. It was a wall of Macs. McCoist, McKimmie, McCall and MacLeod. In our rush, I was stood where Murdo was supposed to be, and vice-versa, and when the left-back, Branco, a player known for possessing dynamite in his boots, smashed the ball into Murdo's kisser (I can still hear the thud), the wee man went down. It took a considerable amount of smelling salts to wake him up.

As he was being stretchered off, showing signs of life, I walked over and shouted, 'Murdo, are you all right, pal?'

Murdo lifted his head slightly, and gave me a half-hearted thumbs up.

'Pal, you need to look on the bright side,' I said.

'Bright side?'

'Aye, that coulda been me!'

In the second half, the lads on the bench had one ear on what was happening between Costa Rica and Sweden, and with the Swedes winning, our possible draw would be enough. I came off with a quarter of an hour to go, and as a squad we dared to dream. And then disaster struck. The Brazilian midfielder, Alemão, struck from twenty yards. His shot had some venom to it, but it was one that our goalkeeper Jim Leighton would usually have hoped to cling on to or put behind for a corner. Instead, the ball squirmed from his hands, he and Gary Gillespie did their best to thwart the onrushing Careca, but the young striker Müller was gifted an empty net, and with that, all was lost.

I felt so sorry for Jim. Just weeks before he had been dropped from the English FA Cup final by Alex Ferguson, a decision that left him understandably distraught, and now he'd made an error that would invite even more scrutiny. A keeper's life is a tough one. Jim had made several brilliant saves to keep the game goalless and our dreams alive, but then one lapse and it's lights out. To rub salt into his and our wounds, the Brazilian Taffarel made a magnificent save to deny Mo a late equaliser. We were going home.

It's strange leaving a group after a long (not long enough) and intense spell of living and working with each other. Suddenly it is all over, you fly home, say your goodbyes and head back to normality. Only, it didn't quite work out like that for me. With the farewells done, I headed to my house, only to realise that, the whole of my family having flown out for the Brazil match, they were still sunning themselves in Italy, and I had not packed a key.

After the disappointment of my first tournament and knowing that my family were all sat poolside sipping on piña coladas, whilst I was standing in the pissing rain in East Kilbride, I called my old pal Knoxy and ask to stay in his spare room for a couple of nights. Knoxy was very welcoming.

'They've locked you out, have they, Coisty?' he said. 'Changed the locks on you, have they, Coisty? I didnae think you played tha' bad, pal.'

Once my folks eventually allowed me back into the family home, international football came around quickly with qualification for the 1992 European Championships getting off to a great start with a 2–1 win at Hampden over Romania. They were a more than up-and-coming side, housing future household names such as Hagi, Popescu and Petrescu. They took the lead, but a first-half equaliser from Hearts' John Robertson got us back in it (from a headed assist by yours truly that Joe Jordan would have been proud of, by the way), before I scored a cracker from two yards to win us the game.

It must have been a good goal, because decades later,

strolling through a German hotel lobby whilst covering the 2024 European Championships, I heard 'McCoist!' I turned around and it was two Romanian journalists, who recalled the games and the goals, and were after a selfie. Football is beautiful like that.

We'd made a great start to qualifying, and we backed it up with another home win against Switzerland and a 1–1 draw out in Bulgaria, another side going places and possessing Hristo Stoichkov in its attack. I was pleased for Andy Roxburgh. He had taken a lot of stick, especially after the Costa Rica defeat, but with plenty of new, fresh faces, his team had performed brilliantly for him in the qualifying group. To win the group that possessed such strength proved there was much more to him than some had suggested. Being the first manager to lead our country to a European Championships certainly silenced some of the sceptics.

The squad remained similar to the one that had travelled to Italy, with a few tweaks. Andy Goram came in as goal-keeper. Jim Leighton would be involved again in the future, and he was certainly too strong a character to remain despondent after 1990. But Andy was a brilliant keeper as well and from 1991 he became my teammate at Rangers.

Andy had come from Hibernian, and shortly after his arrival, we played Hibs in the semi-final of the League Cup at Hampden. They beat us one-nothing, and the following day, we were all sat in the training ground dressing room, still feeling very down by the defeat. The goalie walked in and sat down.

'Fuckin' typical,' he said. 'If I'd stayed at Hibs, I'd be in a cup final.'

'Fuckin' typical?' I replied. 'If you'd stayed at Hibs, *we'd* be in a cup final!'

Andy was a great lad, one hundred miles an hour. A real character. I cannot confirm this, but there was a great story about a time when a girl was said to have come to the goalie's room, and she was carrying a cake. Craig Brown, by now the manager, had got wind of this highly frowned upon visit and headed straight to the room. He burst in and there she was with the cake. The goalie was trying to look blameless as Browny asked the young lady, in no uncertain terms, what she was doing there.

'I'm delivering Andy's birthday cake,' she replied innocently.

Browny supposedly left the room, got on the phone to someone at the SFA, asked Andy's date of birth and got it. Then he stormed back into Andy's room and said to the lady, 'I'm afraid you're six months too late!'

Having qualified, one of only eight clubs to make the finals, we rightly felt good about our chances, albeit knowing we had to find a way through a group including Germany, the holders Holland and Russia. I was certainly flying at Rangers. We won our fourth title in a row in 1992, I managed to score thirty-nine goals, won the players' player of the year, the Scottish Football Writers' player of the year, and the European Golden Boot for my thirty-four league goals.

I felt great. I was playing with complete freedom and going into games not just thinking I'd score a goal, but knowing I'd get two. My confidence was sky high in my own game and in those around me. Sports people are often asked about being in 'the zone'. I don't know much about that, but in those first seasons of the 1990s, I do know that everything seemed aligned, both physically and mentally.

Life, however, does have a way of reminding you of its fragility. The national team had headed to North America for some warm-up games. It was a decision that raised eyebrows. Why travel so far away for an upcoming tournament that was relatively close to home? Andy's thoughts were that he wanted us to get away from prying eyes, from the outside pressures that come with pre-tournament life. He also wanted his new squad to bond, which we did.

We had a win against the USA in Denver before beating Canada in Toronto, and it was there in our hotel that I received the news about my wee granny, Jeanie. I was rooming with Richard Gough, and when the phone rang, Goughie answered it and I could tell by the big man's persona that it was bad news from home. It was my mum on the phone. 'Hello, Mrs McCoist,' Goughie said. And then a pause. Something wasn't right. Goughie was not being his usual engaging self.

'Yes, Mrs McCoist, I'll put him on.'

He handed me the phone, but I knew what I was about to hear.

Losing Jeanie was incredibly hard for my family. My mum was distraught at losing this incredible woman, who had worked so hard to give her and her siblings a loving life. I had lost a granny who meant everything to me. My only grandparent, a champion for everything I achieved, a constant voice on the end of the phone. Quiet, unassuming, loving and kind; but also able to use all those characteristics to make her the most powerful woman around. To this day, I miss her.

In Sweden, we started our competition with a really good performance against the Dutch in Gothenburg, and we regarded ourselves very unlucky to lose to a late Denis Bergkamp goal. Myself and the Aberdeen full-back Stewart McKimmie felt even unluckier when we were asked to undergo a drug test, which meant waiting around until nature called. Waiting being the operative word.

Poor Stewart had spent ninety valiant minutes chasing and frustrating the likes of Marco van Basten and Ruud Gullit, whilst I had done my best to run in behind Ronald Koeman and Frank Rijkaard. That meant losing a fair amount of sweat and so, being asked to fill a specimen container took a bit of patience.

Patience that our management team seemingly didn't have. Having put their heads around the corner to find Stewart and myself sat with a couple of the Dutch lads, all four of us in the same predicament, they said, 'Hurry up, we have a flight to catch.' Hurry up? If only it was that easy. We were drinking gallons of water, but still no joy.

Eventually, they left us, and so we ordered a crate of beers and sat talking football with our new Dutch pals, before heading back to the hotel and enjoying a couple more beers with the fans. It certainly took the edge off the defeat.

Our next two games were in the city of Norrköping. A beautiful place in the far north of Sweden, where the nights are short, but we filled the time as ever with a combination of table tennis, pool, card schools and films. Once again we were able to choose from an array of movies, but with the wonderful Pat Nevin amongst us, there were conflicting tastes. Most of us would ask for the latest Arnold Schwarzenegger action movie, whilst the wee man was more likely to be keen on a black and white avant-garde film with subtitles.

I love Pat. The problem he had hanging around with us boys was that his brains are in his head, whilst ours were in our boots. Actually, he had brains in his head *and* boots, as he was some player, and I would love being away with him and chatting about music, a subject he knows so much about.

Buoyed by our performance against Holland, we played very well in our second game against Germany. Myself and Jukebox Durie worked hard, as did the rest of the lads, but were undone 2–0 by the world champions, who just knew how to get things done.

Lothar Matthäus was injured, but facing Jürgen Kohler, Guido Buchwald, Stefan Effenberg, Thomas Hassler, Matthias Sammer, Andreas Möller, Andreas Brehme, Jürgen Klinsmann and Karl-Heinz Riedle was going to offer us challenges. I think on paper that German team, which went on to lose the final against Denmark, was better than the one that won the tournament in England four years later. We had a very good go. Andy would cite the fact that we had thirteen corners to their two, but one good goal from Riedle and a deflected cross from Effenberg did us.

It meant that we had nothing to play for, but despite the Russians having drawn both their games and needing to win to progress, we put on one of our finest displays and beat a very good side 3–0. You could argue that it was too little, too late, but it underlined what a good group of players we had. Typically though, it wasn't enough. *Heroic failures.* Words I hate, but once again they were words that followed us home.

After the match, we had a night in Norrköping. 'On you all go, have a few beers, enjoy yourselves,' Andy said. So, off we went and found ourselves in a very lively music venue. Feeling raucous, I was soon up on stage with a band, belting out some Bruce Springsteen tracks. I gave it my all singing 'Dancing in the Dark', and after it was done, with a bottle of beer in my hand and sweat rolling down my shirt, I took in the applause (a detail that perhaps only I can confirm) from an equally upbeat crowd.

Suddenly, from the side of the small stage, there was a shout. 'Oh you!' It was the great Archie Knox, one of Andy's coaches, and my assistant manager at Rangers. He was straining his voice to be heard over the speakers and the mayhem going on around us.

'Oh you!'

'Wha' is it, Archie?'

'That's me. I'm headin' back to the hotel.'

'Okay, Archie. See you later.'

'Just one thing . . .'

'Wha' is it?'

'Training starts with the club on Monday, July thirteenth. Ten a.m. Don't be late.'

He went to walk off, leaving me on the stage with the wind firmly taken out of my sails. Archie then turned around and headed back to me.

'Wha' is it now, Archie?'

'And there will be a weight check.'

With that, he was gone.

eight

THE TARTAN ARMY

T HE people. In the end, it's all about the people. I was so lucky to play football professionally for over two decades, and there are so many wonderful memories that come with playing for clubs and country, but an enduring factor is the crowd that we do it in front of, and none come with more passion and personality than the Tartan Army. A set of fans so loved and so well known, they even have their own name.

These are the fans who, by fair means and sometimes foul, have got into stadiums all over the world, with a desire to see their country try to win football matches as unquenched as their seemingly never-ending thirst. Such has been the fervour with which they do it, they are perhaps even more famous than the players who have pulled on the blue shirt.

It's difficult to put into words what playing in front of such passionate fans is like. When I first started, with no official national anthem, songs such as 'Scotland the Brave' were used to rouse the spirits, and then towards the end of my international career, 'Flower of Scotland' came into play. To be honest, stood in a line with your pals and about to represent your country, they could play anything – Ultravox, Proclaimers, Bay City Rollers – you are so ready to run through walls for that crowd, most things will get you going.

Today, the Tartan Army has made their rendition of 'Flower of Scotland' every bit as exhilarating as the rugby crowd at Murrayfield, and that is the biggest compliment I can give them. Hampden has always been a rousing place to play football, especially when I started in the early 1990s with about 74,000 in that huge bowl, but as a player, you do also appreciate the opponents.

Don't get me wrong, nothing beats the roar of the Tartan Army, but I remember being lined up in Paris before a game and 'La Marseillaise' began, and then the ground was rocking as the revolutionary song was being belted out. I whispered in Mo Johnston's ear next to me, 'I tell you what, wee man . . .'

'Wha'?'

'This song is an absolute belter.'

Mo nodded his head in agreement, and it was all we could do to stop from tapping our feet.

But, as I say, nothing much beats a floodlit game at Hampden, on a frosty Scottish evening pierced by the sound of tens of thousands of voices with patriotism and glory on their minds. So loud, it might even be a distraction. A sound like thunder from the gods might be enough to sidetrack us mere mortal footballers, but fortunately, when it came to scoring or trying to score, I was able to shut the noise out.

I had it from a fairly young age, when the sound was more like three men chatting in the background at Alloa than the roar of 74,000 at Hampden, but be it a one-on-one situation, or a snap shot at goal, there would suddenly be silence in my head. Maybe it's a strikers' thing, being able to close off the outside world, but then if I was lucky enough to score, there was that noise again, that guttural eruption of shared joy, and other than the sound of the laughter of my kids, I might never have heard anything better.

That's why I say it's all about the people. It was big Jock Stein who rightly said that football was nothing without fans, and it is their presence and their support and their sheer emotion that makes it all so much more memorable.

Two of the most memorable moments of my international career involved me and the crowd. One was my goal against Greece that helped us to qualify for the 1996 European Championships. The goal itself was special to me, and when I saw my header glide in slow motion past the keeper and into the far corner, my natural instinct was to be near the supporters. I was off, hurdling those advertising boards, slightly concerned that wee John Robertson might struggle should he follow me, because being near the delirium is what it's all about.

There was also that game against Switzerland at Villa Park, in those 1996 Euros. I remember warming up and in the crowd, behind the goal where I would score, I saw an old schoolmate, Ian Buchanan. I used to play football with Buch for Hunter High and I remember a great strike he had in a big school match that hit the bar and I scored from the rebound – and now there he was right in with the Tartan

Army. We acknowledged each other and it reminded me just how lucky I was to be playing for my country, and whilst I'm out there in the kit, those who have travelled to support us have come from the same places as me, with the same backgrounds.

I certainly used to be in the stands with them. My first game watching the national team was a 2–0 win over England in Glasgow. I remember the walk to Hampden and being around the older guys, knowing not to talk but to listen, to take in their thoughts about the game, the players, and of course the English.

I can recall being enthralled by the sheer number of people. My friend and I had sneaked out of our houses and onto a train, and managed to get lifted into the stand to join over 120,000 supporters for the 1973 Cup final between Celtic and Rangers. That day was an eye-opener for a ten-year-old, but then to be there a year later, this time with the Scottish international fans, I remember being hypnotised by the sea of yellow Lion Rampant flags, and revelling in the sheer magnitude of a nation united in passion.

My first away trip with the national team was in 1979, when me and my pal Knoxy travelled south for a game at Wembley. We stayed with Knoxy's family in north-west London, but I remember the train going down getting fuller and fuller at every stop and the noise getting louder and louder, until the train was shaking as we pulled into Euston.

We lost the game 3–1, but like on so many of these occasions, the two hours spent in the stadium was just a bullet point in an adventure that included the fountains in Trafalgar Square being filled with both lager and Scotsmen showing off their far from synchronised swimming skills. It was a day shared with thousands of kindred spirits with a combined goal for their weekend: to drink, laugh and let the nation's capital both see and hear them in their full glory.

By then, I was playing professional football with St Johnstone, but I would be lying if I said I was stood on those Wembley terraces, thinking to myself that I would one day be playing for the Tartan Army. I was doing all right, scoring some goals in the lower leagues, but I certainly wasn't being touted as a future centre forward with the national team. No, as Knoxy and myself joined the train home the following day, a train still lively but not as bouncing as twenty-four hours earlier, my hungover thoughts were only about a life with the national team to be lived from the terraces.

London will probably have been pleased to see the back of us that day, but whilst Trafalgar Square might have needed a wee spring clean, it was nothing like the outcry that came after that notorious fixture two years earlier, when thousands of Scottish fans celebrated a famous win on the Wembley pitch and their high jubilation turned into what some English folk described as basic vandalism.

With a level of infamy guaranteed after that day in England, the Tartan Army went global in 1978, when they travelled in their thousands to Argentina for a World Cup in which the team drastically underachieved, but the people of our nation made themselves very much known, loved and remembered.

There are hundreds of stories of fans selling washing machines and cars, even looking for a good price for their kids, just to try and get out to South America. Fans were turning up in Canada, only to realise that they still had a wee way to go, and eventually the nation of Argentina was greeted every morning with a new influx of these strange men in kilts and tammies, arriving on trains, or having hitched lifts and on bicycles.

There is one story about the guys who somehow got a lift on a submarine. I can't confirm if it is true, but I think it has to be and until my dying day, I will laugh at the idea of a group of Scotsmen who got as far as the Azores before talking their way onto a passing sub. As the days went by, upping the periscope, one of them turned and said, 'Hey, fellas, get the last of those tinnies open, we've almost made it.' I love it, and the very fact that I think it must be true says everything about the Scots' sheer determination to be at the match, and to be in and around an international tournament.

Things change in life and in football, but one thing remains the same, and that is the numbers that Scotland take to international occasions, and the humour with which they do it. The fashions might change, the feather haircuts and bellbottoms of my early days are no longer around, but those who make the journeys do so with the same wit and resolve.

Back in the late 1970s and 1980s, when hooliganism was very much a problem in the game, those that followed Scotland abroad seemed to distance themselves from it. England's problems with trouble abroad were very much publicised, and I have a theory that it was because of that, the Tartan Army policed themselves. 'If other fans are known for causing trouble, then we are going to be the exact opposite.' Stubborn and cantankerous to the end.

Don't get me wrong, there was trouble in some quarters of the Scottish game. I was at Hampden in 1980 for the Cup final between Rangers and Celtic and witnessed running battles between the fans on the pitch, like I'd never seen before, but when it came to the national team, travelling supporters took the view that yes, drink would be taken, but the only damage would be to sore heads and livers. It is a policy that has very much stuck.

It is always easy to spot a Scottish football fan abroad, especially in sunnier climes where pale limbs and rosy cheeks are as much part of our national identity as the tartan. To be fair, it's not just the fans. I remember having the honour of being asked to play in a game for Luis Figo's charity out in the Algarve, back in 2004. There were big names everywhere, Sir Alex Ferguson took the team I was playing for, the original Ronaldo came along, Gazza was there and Rui Costa, up front we had Michael Schumacher, and whilst I was playing, on came an almost seventy-year-old Bobby Charlton.

I can report that even then Bobby was still a special footballer, but it was afterwards I was in the shower, and I could hear some of these superstars laughing.

A wee bit concerned, I thought, are they laughing at me? The laughing continued.

'Ally,' they said.

'Aye, wha' is it?'

'Do you like golf?'

Strange question, I thought, especially in the circumstances, but I nodded and said, 'Aye, aye I do. Love it.'

They all began to laugh.

'Why? Wha' of it?'

They stopped sniggering and gestured to my arms and my legs. What they were laughing at were my red or almost tanned arms and legs – the sort of Scottish suntan that must only have been forged out on the golf course.

My chance to make the leap from international punter to international striker came in 1986, and whilst my debut was that friendly out in Holland, it was some six months later that I made my first appearance for my country at Hampden. Luxembourg might not have been the most illustrious opposition, but the occasion was given a sense of historical importance in that it was the last of Kenny Dalglish's 102 caps. To me, just being out on the same pitch as my idol was something not to be forgotten, but on top of that, I was there not only representing my country, but doing it in the old stadium that I had visited so many times with my father and with my pals.

I immediately wanted more. It's just different playing for your country. Pure pride. My thoughts turned naturally to the many people who played such big parts in helping me get there. My relationship with the Tartan Army itself always seemed to be a positive one. There was no ill-feeling towards us Old Firm players, in fact, I can only recall one occasion that the fans turned on any of us, when Gary McAllister got some stick for his form. It stood out for two reasons. One was that Gary Mac was always that good and never deserved any sort of stick, and the other because it was just so rare to hear.

My first goal for my country took six games, but never were there any signs of discontent from the supporters. Just the usual backing that helped me feel like I belonged. With all that great support, the feeling that rushed over me when I scored my first goal against Hungary at Hampden in September 1987 (an effort that was followed just half an hour later with my second) was pure euphoria. Tick, I'd played for Scotland. Tick, now I've scored. Magic.

When you score for Scotland and you run to that crowd, you can see the people, and as I say, those faces in the throng are very much like ours, especially back then. We were athletes, but times were a wee bit different, and even the great players might have the odd vice or two. I remember being away with the squad. We were in a hotel room, myself, wee Mo Johnston and Steve Nicol.

Stevie was some lad, a great player and a great character. We were all playing cards in the room, and every now and then, every half an hour or so, he would put his cards down, go over to the bed, get on the phone to room service and simply say, 'Same again.'

Then, some ten minutes later there would be a knock on the door, and in would come a tray with four things on it. A pint of lager, a packet of salt and vinegar crisps, a single cigarette and a Swan Vesta match. That was it. Now you can't get more simple or man of the people than that, can you?

Away at tournaments, we might be left to live in our hotel bubble, but that wouldn't bother the fans. Scottish football fans could blag their way into Fort Knox and leave calmly with a bar or two of the good stuff. In places such as Italy, staying in our beautiful coastal hotel, a few of us would be enjoying some downtime by the swimming pool when suddenly blocking out the sun would be three burly lads from Aberdeen. 'All right, boys?' they'd ask. 'Where's the bar?'

Sweden in 1992 was the same. I always laugh at the image of this beautiful Swedish policewoman in an embrace with a fairly well-oiled Scot, his beard in full growth, his breath no doubt propelled by whisky. That was the tournament when myself and Stewart McKimmie were held back in our Gothenburg hotel after a drugs test, and whilst the squad flew back to our northern base, we had to stay put.

Andy Roxburgh must have heard the news that two of his players would be absent, and one of them was me, and screamed blue murder. Luckily, Stewart was one of the nicest men in the squad but also one of the most sensible, so any thoughts of a raucous night out on the town were somewhat tempered.

What did happen back in our hotel, though, was rare and memorable. The place was full of Scottish fans, and so to sit and mingle with them, to listen to their stories and hear about the laughs they were having travelling around the country watching us, only underlined how vital they are to everything. Andy might have had a sleepless night wondering what his number 9 was up to, alone in a faraway Swedish city, but he needn't have worried. Whilst it is true that the lads we met were very keen to buy us drinks, and whilst it may also be true that many of them succeeded, Stewie and I were up in our beds at a more than healthy hour.

That was over thirty years ago, and today I am blessed, not only because of the sixty-one times I ran out in a Scotland kit to play for those fans, but also in the fact that through my work, I still get to travel the world and see once again the humour, fun and dedication to a party that they have always brought to footballing occasions.

Us players might get the plaudits, we might get our names in the odd history book, but we know it is the people we do it for that really count.

nine

STILL DREAMING

IT is the spring of 1993. We've been battered and now the manager is on the receiving end of his own onslaught. It's a defeat that means Scotland, for the first time in almost a quarter of a century, will not be going to the World Cup. Portugal have done us 5–0 in Lisbon, the press smell blood, and Andy Roxburgh is in the firing line. It's the heaviest defeat since England beat us 5–0 in 1973, and the heaviest defeat to a non-British side since the Uruguayans beat us 7–0 at the 1954 World Cup; facts and figures that are being put to the manager. Pondering what he has just witnessed, Andy concludes, 'A team died out there tonight.'

Whilst he was facing the press, I was facing a long lay-off. I had enjoyed a fantastic season, scoring forty-nine goals, and with several games left of the domestic campaign, I was confident of cracking the fifty mark. My goals helped Rangers to a domestic treble, and only a week earlier we had played the last of an unbeaten campaign in a new-look Champions League, counting ourselves desperately unlucky not to make the final.

That night in Lisbon's Stadium of Light, like my team-mates, I had been left in darkness, and the mood following our defeat was compounded by my leg being in absolute agony. Late in the game, having had a proper run-in with their big centre-half, Jorge Costa, I went to smash the ball, caught a defender and was left in agony. Hugh Allan, the physio, came on but as he was treating me, I saw Costa with a slight grin on his face. As if he was enjoying my woe. 'Right, Hugh, get me up,' I said. 'I do not want that bastar' to know how much I'm hurtin'.'

Hugh helped me up, I put weight on the leg, and my mind was changed. 'Right, Hugh, get me off.' I knew it was a bad one, and lying on the treatment table in a dressing room drowning in solemn silence, my mind switched back to a happier time in Portugal.

It was 1983. I was on my holidays in the Algarve and enjoying a beer in the bar. A local gentleman came over, very Portuguese-looking with a huge moustache, and we got to talking about football. He had no idea that I was a professional back home, but he invited me to come along to watch, and possibly play in a little seven-a-side match he was involved in. I'd brought my boots, so why not?

When he left, the barman asked me if I knew who that was. I said no, but he seemed very nice. The barman smiled and said no more about it. The following day, the gentleman took me along to the pitch, and I was quickly aware that there were far more people than I would expect for a local kick-about. Then I saw a sign: 'BENFICA vs ALGARVE SELECT XI.'

The guy walked me into the small community stadium and into the Benfica dressing room. There he introduced me to the guys and we went out, I scored, we won and the crowd went mad. It was only after the game I realised that amongst my great new teammates were Carlos Manuel, who would score a winner against England in the 1986 World Cup, and Frederico, who left Benfica that year for Boavista, where I played against him for Rangers. We remained great pals until his death in 2019.

As for the man who invited me, I discovered after the match he was Humberto Coelho, a star of the Portuguese game, at the time still on the books at Benfica, and in a couple of decades, a successful manager of the national team. Afterwards I told them that I was a player at Rangers in Glasgow, and we all fell about laughing. For the remainder of my holiday, the guys took me under their wing and we all enjoyed the best of times together.

Back in the Stadium of Light, I was awoken from my trip down memory lane by the pain in my leg. The team's doctor, a great man called Dr Stewart Hillis, saw I was hurting and told me that I had two options, a hospital in Lisbon or back to Glasgow. I wanted to get away. 'Let's take our chances,' I said. 'Let's get home.'

The doctor insisted that we wait for a bit. The team had packed up and left, but the doctor wanted me to let the crowds go first and then some time after full-time, he organised an ambulance. As I was walking along on crutches through the bowels of the stadium, standing by the ambulance were Carlos Manuel, Frederico and Humberto Coelho. All three had been at the game, seen that I was hurt, and hung about to say hello and check I was okay. Amazing. I will never forget how much better I felt after seeing their smiling faces.

It was a fleeting reunion and a brief respite from the pain I was in. Having been whisked away by the doctor in the ambulance and fast-tracked through the airport, the doctor and I were told to wait on the side of the runway whilst the squad's plane was readied. It was a surreal moment, but a painful one.

'How bad?' the doctor asked.

'Really bad, doc. Fuckin' agony, in fact.'

He then broke it to me that the team had left with all his stuff, and therefore he had nothing in the way of painkillers for me. More swear words. He said, 'I do have some duty-free though,' and produced a bagful of wine. 'Fuckin' crack them open,' I cried. Never has the term 'for medicinal reasons' meant so much when drinking. The doctor got the bottles open and in a very short period of time, the two of us polished off a couple of bottles of red.

I was stretchered up into the plane and, seeing me in quite a state, the boys gave me stick. 'I'll be fit for Saturday!' I screamed back. I'm surprised I didn't offer to fly the plane. Maybe I did. Back in Glasgow, the doctors at the hospital told me what I already knew, I had broken my leg, but the good news was that it was the cleanest of breaks.

They showed me the X-ray and it was a clean, straight line, as if someone had taken a ruler to it. Walter Smith then arrived at the hospital, typically caring and supportive, and whilst I was out for the rest of the season, I worked my hardest to get back to fitness. By the following autumn I was back playing.

My big inspiration had been my pal Ian Durrant, who got through his terrible injury in 1988 with a work ethic I had never seen before. Even when I was injured, some five years later, he was still in the gym every day working on his quads to maintain support around the knee. I took it on myself to get in there and work just like him. I may even have overdone it with the weights, as I became a bit too top heavy, but the leg healed and I was able to play almost thirty games that season with a goal tally that got into double figures.

I wouldn't play for Scotland though for over two years. Having told the press in Portugal that they had witnessed the death of his team, it wasn't long before Andy Roxburgh departed from the national team's managerial office. His replacement was his assistant, Craig Brown, and so the transition was a seamless one.

Browny was a great guy. He had us all in stitches, sometimes unintentionally. We even found the funny side of something he did during that ill-fated visit to Portugal in 1993. The night before the match, we were having a team meeting, when Browny got very excited. He told us that the Portuguese were likely to play Rui Barros, who was the attacking midfielder at Monaco at the time, but soon headed back to Porto.

He was talented, but Browny had some inside information. 'They are going to play him, but I've just been in a taxi and my driver reckons the wee man is too small.' We were all staring at him, and he went on. 'They're going to play him, but we have nothing to worry about. The driver is adamant, he's too small.'

We started to crack up laughing and Browny stopped, got the hump, and said, 'What are you laughing at? I'm telling you, I'm telling you, he's that small!' Browny then pointed to a table in the room. 'In fact,' he said, 'he could walk under that table with a top hat on.' We were falling about the place and Browny had no idea how funny he was being. The following night, the smiles were wiped from our faces when wee Rui Barros scored two of his team's five goals.

I returned in the August of 1995 for a crunch tie against Greece at Hampden. A qualifying match for the following summer's European Championships in England. Russia were leading the group, and in second place, it was tight between ourselves and Greece. We really needed to avoid defeat against a team who had already beaten us in Athens.

I was on the bench, but just thrilled to be back in the squad, and watched intently as a tense game unfolded. Then, in the seventy-first minute, Browny told me to get warm, I was going on for Duncan Shearer. It was a great feeling to have the blue shirt on my back again, and as I got on, I had the usual thoughts. Get a nice early touch, be willing, run the channels, make things difficult. A minute later, I was sprinting to the jubilant home supporters, because I'd scored the winning goal.

Having worked hard to get back from my broken leg, and watched from afar as they made strides to reach another major tournament, the feeling of euphoric joy I got from that goal might not have been bettered throughout my career. It was a great goal in many ways. The ball was on the right and John Collins, with his always sweet left foot, swung the ball in. I managed to step back, got the defender off balance, then darted across him and with only the merest of glancing headers, I watched as it glided into the far left-hand corner. I was away. Hurdling the advertising hoards like Red Rum over the fences at Aintree, and making my way towards the punters with a smile beaming across my face.

It was a huge win, one that gave us breathing space, and two more wins against Finland and San Marino meant we were headed over the border to another Euros with a talented squad, working alongside a manager whom we all liked very much. We couldn't wait to get down there.

Browny was great at encouraging fun. He liked his teams to be enjoying themselves. We had to get the work done, but if that came with the sound of laughter, so much the better. Even if that laugh was sometimes at his own expense. Browny had this slight limp, and would stroll onto the training pitch with a bag of balls over his shoulder. Wee John Spencer, a great lad and very funny, would do a great impression of the manager. He'd flick the bag of balls onto his back and then mimic Browny's walk, putting the cones down, whilst we all cracked up.

When the manager saw it, and how much of a laugh it got, he would throw the bag of balls at John and ask him to do the impression, knowing it would get the session off to a happy start.

I got on very well with Browny. How could I not, especially that year? In March 1996, Browny gave me the captaincy for a game against Australia at Hampden. Sure, it was to mark my fiftieth cap, but still, the pride I had in wearing the armband and leading the lads out onto the famous pitch was right up there with the greatest moments of my life.

It's hard to explain. You think of your parents. My dad had died two years earlier, but to have the national team walking out behind me put him uppermost in my thoughts. He had been there when I was a young semi-pro, taking me on trains and buses to get me up to Perth and back, always encouraging, always a presence. I wondered what he and my granny Jeanie would have felt. Two people who helped me so much throughout my young life, but were no longer with me to see it. I thought of my mum, up in the stands, thinking of them too and the pride she must be feeling.

I thought of the coaches who had taken my young sides, the men at Calderwood Stars, giving up their time so I could learn the game and try to excel in it. I thought about Archie Robertson at my high school and Norrie Cranston, the manager at Fir Park boys. I thought of all my managers and all my teammates. I was captain of Scotland. What could be better?

I have a photo of me that night, which I cherish, having captained Scotland and with my oldest boy, Alexander, in my arms. He would have been just one year old, and for one of my kids to have been there meant so much. It still does.

I even scored the only goal of the game that night, past Australia's Mark Bosnich, who to this day says he let it in because it was my fiftieth cap. It was a magic night, one that I will never forget.

Having scored twenty goals for Rangers that season, I was happy with my form. My fitness had been a concern after a calf injury kept me out of the Scottish Cup final, but Browny had called me to say he would give me all the time he could to get fit, for which I was very grateful.

I didn't expect to start every game. We had another set of fine strikers. Gordon Durie was with me at Rangers now and we had hit it off. Also with us were Kevin Gallagher, who was playing well at Blackburn, Scott Booth doing great at Aberdeen, and John Spencer, who was scoring goals at Chelsea. We were, though, unlucky to lose big Duncan Ferguson, who had to have a hernia operation.

The big fella had made his debut in 1992 and come with us to the European Championships in Sweden. I had liked him immediately. He is nothing like his hard-man image suggests, and I have always had time for him. What happened with him and the SFA was very avoidable, in my opinion. I could appreciate Duncan's decision to refuse to play for Scotland, after he had served jail time for assault in 1995 and he felt aggrieved at the length of the twelve-match ban served on him by the association. The SFA could have been seen to take the appropriate action, whilst also supporting the player back into the international fold. In the end there were only losers.

I had an early reason to have my own grievances with Dunc. He beat me at cards, and took a nice bit of cash from my wallet. We were away with Scotland, the trip in North America prior to the 1992 Euros. It was Dunc's first and he's shyer than he looks. He wouldn't say boo to a goose, but after his victory at cards, he found his voice. Having failed to win any of it back, I made the mistake of falling asleep on the plane.

Duncan was looking at me sleeping and started waving the money in my face, shouting, 'Look at me, lads, look at this. I remember back in the day, I used to be in awe of this man, but look at me now, I'm waving money in his face and I'm laughing!'

Everyone was in hysterics, but I had some sort of revenge when he bought himself, with my money, a homing pigeon and called it 'Coisty'. Dunc loves his pigeons, but having released my namesake for his maiden voyage out of the loft, the bird fucked off and never returned. To be fair, the big man should have known better. Naming a pigeon after me and expecting it to be reliably punctual was a foolhardy venture and he got what he deserved.

With his injury, we all felt for the big man and he would have been a vital asset to the squad. Despite that we headed to another North American tour prior to the Euro 1996 championships, full of energy and hope. Browny must have noted how much we benefited as a group from the similar trip in 1992, so we played two friendlies, and despite two defeats to the USA and Colombia, it was a good trip.

The bond was evident on the day we departed for America. I had been carrying a knock. On the eve of the Scottish Cup final against Hearts, I had been nursing that calf strain. I'd got fit, but it went again in the warm-up. Looking back, as distraught as I was, it was hilarious. Durranty had been told he wasn't involved that day, so had headed up to get a good spot in the players' bar and was onto his second can of Tennent's. I let Walter know that I wasn't able to play and he sent Davie Dodds, the first-team coach, running up to see the wee man. 'Hey, you!' he shouted at Durranty as he sipped on his can. 'Put that down, Coisty's done his calf, you're in!' Durranty still boasts that he is the only player in history to play in the Cup final with a can and a half of lager in him.

The following day, I headed to the airport to travel with the national team to the States. The SFA had decided that with a limited number of business class seats, those players with the most caps should take them. This meant that the likes of myself, Gary McAllister and Jukebox Durie were in relative luxury, enjoying a game of cards and a glass of wine. Meanwhile, Eoin Jess, Craig Burley and John Spencer, amongst others, were sat tight back in economy, only to be visited regularly with one of our faces popping through the curtains, with a smile and 'Get it up yer, lads!' After a while, when I had visited for around the tenth time, wee John could be heard saying calmly, 'It's nae funny, Coisty.'

Juvenile larks at 35,000 feet aside, the squad were a close unit. Gary Mac, my old mate from Fir Park, was one of the most respected players in the English game, a fabulous footballer named captain in a team full of leaders. Alongside him in midfield was John Collins, another beautiful player, who had moved abroad and now played for and lived in Monaco. It was a place that suited him. Cool, slick and lavish, John always had the look of a player who could thrive abroad. Some players, myself very much included, just look right for the Scottish game, but with his cultured left-peg, John was always destined for foreign climes.

At centre-half, we had Colin Hendry, the most Scottish of Scotsmen. He was from so far north in the country, we joked that he was closer to Reykjavik than Hampden. The big man was brilliant to have around. A man who woke up singing 'Flower of Scotland' and, at the time, was one of the best defenders in Britain. He was born to play for Scotland.

We went into the Euro '96 competition, as ever, hopeful of progress. Holland, England and Switzerland were all fancied ahead of us, but there was a quiet air of confidence about us, which was justified after a determined goalless draw against the Dutch at Villa Park.

England were next, and all of us were happy to tell the brilliant staff at our hotel that we fancied beating their boys. Why not? England were under pressure. They had drawn with Switzerland in their opening game, and the public and press were still unhappy with the images taken in Hong Kong during a pre-tournament tour. Photos of Paul Gascoigne in the notorious dentist chair, having tequila poured down his gullet ('I only went in for a filling,' he said later), were not in line with the new modes of sports nutrition coming into the game. We felt that if we could make life difficult for them, they might crack under the pressure.

I was on the bench, and enjoyed a first half in which we did everything asked of us, upsetting their rhythm whilst looking dangerous on the ball. At halftime England made a tactical change, bringing on Jamie Redknapp, who made a difference to the tempo of the game, to be fair, getting England on the ball and using his passing ability to maintain their possession.

The English went 1–0 up through Alan Shearer, but we were never dismayed, and when Tony Adams brought down Jukebox with what looked like a tired challenge, I really thought, we're going to go on and win this. Gary Mac was on penalties. I had come on by now, but there was no talk of anyone but Gary taking it.

I fully expected him to score and he couldn't have it hit any cleaner, it's just that David Seaman pulled off a fantastic save. Nine times out of ten, it would have gone in, but not today and our hopes were dashed. Yes, I am aware that Uri Geller suggests that from a helicopter above the stadium, he used some of his mystical powers to move the ball, and yes, the ball did move as Gary stepped up, but any talk of magic annoys me to this day.

It was hard enough trying to deal with Gazza's sorcery, let alone Geller's. A minute after Gary's penalty miss, I had an annoyingly perfect view of my Rangers teammate surging forward with one of his powerful runs from midfield, latching on to Darren Anderton's delicate pass, and somehow flicking the ball over big Colin Hendry, who slipped, before unleashing the perfect volley past Goram.

I can see it all unfolding in front of my sad eyes. The move is a piece of genius from a player willing and able to try something on the international stage that most would only try on the playground. The ball goes over Colin's head and I know that it's a clean volley and it is 2–0, and I am praying not to see the net bulge. For 0.002 seconds there is hope, but then it's in, and the game has gone from us.

It all happened so quickly, and despite seeing him do things like that constantly in training, I was left on the half-way line stunned and gutted in equal measure. There could be no surprise when Gazza made light of the dentist chair affair by having his teammates squirt energy drinks into his mouth. As iconic a celebration as it was, I did not see the funny side then, and almost thirty-years later, I'd like to say that time heals, but I'd be lying.

I do cherish a photo of myself and Gazza after the game, though, embracing and swapping shirts. We had agreed to do so before the game but, as ever, he was in demand. I didn't know that our Rangers teammate Stuart McCall had also agreed to swap with Gazza, and at halftime, with all the seriousness of the game we were playing around him, Gazza gave Stuart his shirt in the tunnel, and said, 'Tell Coisty not to worry, he can have my other one after the match.' Typical Gazza.

We had played well, but once again, it was a case of what-ifs. I was rooming with Gary Mac that summer, and it was going to take a lot to lift him. Browny had arranged a few beers that night, a coming together, a chance to get the defeat out of our system with a few drinks and some laughs. The latter would understandably prove hard to get from Gary.

I was down in the bar with the boys, who were all asking after him. I told them that he was taking it bad and that he wasn't coming down. The boys weren't having that. To a man they told me to go up there and get him. They were right. Just as Alan McInally had made light of me being dropped in 1990, the only way to get over disappointment at a tournament is to share it with those in the fight with you.

I went up to the room, told Gary that the boys insisted he come down, that he was their captain, vital to our hopes, and no one blamed him. That night we all had a little drink, the jokes started cracking and Gary was back as the life and soul of the group. Yes, the defeat to the old enemy was a blow, but we still had a chance to go through, and we knew a win against Switzerland might just be enough.

Browny started me at Villa Park, and like all the lads, I was raring to go. What a start to that game. We got into it immediately, buzzing with the roar of our fans, and I had two very good chances to put us one up. The first was an instinctive back-post effort from a corner. I couldn't have done much more and the keeper made a fantastic save. The second one annoyed me. I had pulled away from my marker, and the ball dropped to me in front of goal. I took a decent first touch, but then went for power, when I should have been more composed and placed it in the corner. Watch it back on YouTube and I'm sure you can hear Ian St John, on co-comms, shout, 'Oh, Ally!'

I wasn't going to let those misses get me down. The team were moving the ball around so well, Gary Mac and John Collins getting us forward so quickly, and it was just a case of keeping up with them and stretching the Swiss. About ten minutes before halftime, I nodded the ball down to Gary, made a run around him, screaming for the return pass, and whilst Gary's pass was only about four yards, he weighted it perfectly, and there was nothing else I could do but hit it, and so I did.

When I scored the glancing header against the Greeks the previous summer, I knew it had a chance the minute it left my forehead. This time, I knew it was going places the minute it left my boot's sweet-spot and when it crashed into the top corner, I was away. Against Greece, I was Red Rum jumping the fences at Aintree. This time I was Nijinsky at Epsom, sprinting off into the arms of Browny.

I took a lot of stick for jumping into an embrace with the manager, calling me a teacher's pet. 'What a big sook,' the lads said. 'Oh look, Craigy, I've scored for you!' they said. To be fair, I would have jumped into anyone's arms at that point, such was the pure outpouring of joy at that goal. Browny made a joke of it, saying I didn't run to him to celebrate, but to underline what he'd have got had he picked me in the first two games.

What followed was the strangest of second halves. News started to filter through of England scoring goal after goal against the Dutch, and with each one, the Tartan Army cheered. To see grown men in kilts celebrating an England success was surreal enough, but then the bad news filtered through that Patrick Kluivert had got the most exasperating consolation in the history of football.

Despite laying siege on the Swiss goal, we couldn't get a vital second goal and we were out on goals scored. That is a sucker punch, perhaps the hardest of them all to take. Like 1992, we could take pride in how we had played, but it still wasn't enough.

Afterwards, I stayed in London, at the Radio 1 presenter Chris Evans' house. Chris was a pal and made sure I drowned some sorrows in his north London local, before getting me a ticket for England's quarter-final against Spain on the following Saturday. My obvious hopes for some sort of schaden-freude were dashed by a fortunate penalty shoot-out win for the hosts. It was time to go home.

I remember starting training that July and when Gazza returned, there was no crowing about the result against us. England had been very unlucky not to win the competition, but we fully expected Gazza to return giving us loads about the 2–0 win and maybe even a re-enactment of his goal. Instead there was nothing. No jokes, no flicks and volleys. Sometimes a goal can be that good, there is no need for words. Even Gazza's.

Craig Brown had cemented his place as the national team manager for the World Cup qualification matches, and despite going into my mid-thirties, I hoped to play a part and join the squad at the 1998 tournament in France. I felt fit and played plenty of games for Rangers, getting twenty goals in the 1996/97 season and sixteen the following campaign.

I was involved in several of the successful qualifying matches, and whilst there would be no chance of starting the games in France, I felt strongly that if the team needed a goal from the bench, I was more than capable. Unfortunately, Browny didn't see it that way. I was doing some work in London, when my then wife called me to say the manager had been on the phone, and that it was bad news. I wasn't going. That was that.

It was up there as the biggest blow in my career. I knew I was in the twilight of my career, but I knew I had more to give. I felt fit and sharp, I had scored in the Scottish Cup final, and hoped that my experience would have made me a valuable squad member. I certainly didn't think for one minute that I had some divine right to be picked, but we all back ourselves. That's only natural amongst sportspeople and I didn't greet Browny's decision with a shrug and a smile. It was a painful time.

Years later, Browny gave a speech at a charity dinner. In it, he accepted that he had made a mistake not taking me to France, and thanked me for not publicly making a fuss about it. I would never have done that and to be fair to Browny, he didn't have to explain anything to me or anyone else for making his decision.

After the 1998 World Cup, and more group-stage woe for us Scots, Browny enquired if I would be available to play for the national team again. Apparently he was nervous that I would say no with some hostility. He couldn't have been more wrong. I jumped at the chance to pull on the blue jersey again and happily won my sixtieth and sixty-first caps. The last was a 3–2 victory over Estonia at Tynecastle, a game in which I was replaced late on by Dundee United's Billy Dodds.

As I walked off that afternoon, the Edinburgh sun going down behind me, I had no idea that it would be my final moment as a Scottish international footballer. I am a firm believer that the famous jersey retires you, not the other way around, and I was never going to walk away from it. But that was that. Over a quarter of a century later, I can only look back at my time playing for my country with immense pride, marvel at the players and staff that I shared it all with, and smile at the great laughs we had with one another.

Time moves on, of course, but every now and then, when my phone rings, I allow myself to wonder if someone important saw my six-a-side goal the night before and is calling to offer me my sixty-second cap.

Ach, well, a boy can dream . . . even if most of them have already come true.

ten

WALTER

I N the end, he was everything . . .
It seems ridiculous now to think that for some sixteen years of my life, the name Walter Smith meant nothing to me. Our first encounter was when I was selected to play for the Scotland Under-18s. Walter was the coach and from that moment, it started. A lifetime of roles until he had become everything. My youth team coach, my club's assistant manager, my club's manager, my mentor, my golf rival. I became his assistant at international level, I became his assistant at club level, our wives became friends, he was my (bitter) quiz night rival, he was my second father, and above all, he was my friend. The greatest of friends.

I was lucky enough to play with and for some of the most iconic names in the history of Scottish and British football, but no one outside of my family got close to having more of an impact on me as a player, and a man, than Walter Smith.

Today, just a few years since his death, I can think back to everything Walter became to me, about the times we spent together laughing and chatting, and it brings a smile to my face. To think about Walter is to think about my whole life and when I do so, it reminds me how lucky I've been.

I can be in a dressing room, before a game. Walter, the boss, walks in and we all try to avoid eye contact because we know that if you're dropped, he will give you the eyes, a subtle move of the eyes towards the door, meaning he wants a word and you're not playing.

I can be sat over a dining room table, with a simple but delicious bowl of pasta in front of us, a glass of red wine stood alongside it; Walter's two favourite things and all washed down with the most warming conversation about football, life and everything in-between.

I can be on a golf course, just Walter and myself, marching up the 18th, the scores precariously close, the wind at our backs and the tension rising. There was one such occasion at Loch Lomond, going up the fairway. We're level. It's the week before the Scottish Open, so all the grandstands are out and all sorts of people are preparing.

I've put my second shot just off the green, but with a lot of height on it, the ball lands and it's plugged. Walter's on the green. I shout over.

'The ball is plugged!'

He looks over at me. 'What the fuck d'ya want me to do about it?'

'That's a free drop. It's plugged.'

'You get fuck all free drops. Play it as it lies.'

What with the Open starting, there was this European rules official milling about the place with his clipboards, and Walter clocks him. 'Get him over here.'

'Oi, mate!' I shout. 'Come over here a minute, will ya?'

The fella walks over to us looking confused, Walter is there, and I say, 'You look like you know what you are doing. I'm plugged. That is a free drop, right?'

'Does he, fuck,' Walter says, putting big pressure on the guy.

The bloke takes a look and he says, 'This is a bizarre one. If it happened during a tournament, then yes, it would be lift and a free drop. But, in these normal circumstances, you don't get a free drop, *unless* your playing partner allows it.'

'Wha?!'

The guy repeats it. As he finishes I turn to Walter, and before I can say a word, he's said, 'Don't even fuckin' think about it.'

The bastard makes me play it, beats me by a shot, and is immediately in the 19th and telling everyone who will listen about his victorious round.

When, as a teenager, I first met Walter, I knew immediately I was in the presence of someone who could help my career. It took mere minutes. He started to talk about football and the penny didn't just drop, it clanged to the ground, bounced up and smashed through the ceiling. The man knew football, he understood it thoroughly; he also got footballers, and he could communicate all that knowledge in such a way that made it seem like the simplest thing in the world.

We first met in Monte Carlo, of all places, during a youth tournament out there. I was rooming with big Davie Moyes. Walter was Andy Roxburgh's assistant, and whilst I instantly knew the score regarding Walter's keen grasp for the game we were playing, it would not be long before he cottoned on to the fact that I could be a bit of a wee shite, when I wanted to be.

I was in the room with Moyesie and Walter came in for a chat. I did the old, 'Walter, you have to see the view from our balcony,' so he went to take a look and I locked him out. At first there were a few laughs, but then I could see his expression turning, and it occurred to me that I had made a very big mistake.

What I didn't know then was that Walter was old school. A centre-half with a fondness in his younger days for a wee scrap. At Dundee United, if the mood took him, he would go into a boot room with a few of the boys in there, turn off the lights, and it would be a free-for-all.

So, I'm seeing his face turn red, his smile now a grimace, and I was realising that this very likable man might not be as cuddly as I first thought. He was banging on the balcony window, and it got to the stage that I couldn't let him in because he would kill me. Stalemate. I walked towards the exit, looked at Moyesie, who was thrilled by the turn of events, and told him, don't let him out until I'm at a safe distance. Unfortunately for me, there would be no safe distance, and when Walter caught up with me, I got a good pummelling. The first of a few I took at the hands of my elders and betters in the game.

When not messing about, young footballers had so much to learn from Walter and responded to him. In 1982, alongside Roxburgh, he coached the country's Under-18s to European Championship glory. By then, playing in England with Sunderland, I was very much aware of his abilities and I was not the only one. Working under Jim McLean at Dundee United, and shaping their great team that won domestic honours and reached the 1984 European Cup semi-finals, Walter's reputation grew so much that Alex Ferguson made him his assistant at the 1986 World Cup finals in Mexico.

By the time the Scotland squad were flying back home across the Atlantic that summer, the captain of the team, Graeme Souness, was making plans for my club, Rangers. One of the first things he had negotiated with the club was to bring Walter in from Tannadice as his right-hand man. Us players and our fans, who had been struggling for form, hope and silverware, were in for a treat.

Graeme did not hang around when he became manager at Ibrox. There was no mulling things over, no assessing what he had or what he needed. He jumped straight in and made those huge statement signings I talked about previously, but without a doubt the best thing he did for himself, for the team and ultimately for the football club, was to sanction the appointment of Walter Smith as his number two.

There was no ego to Walter. He was Graeme's assistant, he got that, and so he never thought about manoeuvring into a 'joint-manager' role, but with Graeme also playing for those first couple of seasons, Walter's eyes and knowledge were vital to the instant success that followed. The thing is, Walter was Rangers mad, and everything he did was for the club. His grandfather Jock had made sure of his allegiances, taking him to the ground from their Carmyle home, in Glasgow's

East End; the blue-and-white scarf perhaps not being put on until they got closer to the Copland Road.

Walter, living his own dream at Ibrox, helped make ours come true with his shrewd coaching methods and knowledge of the game. He had been a centre-half in his playing days, and might join in the odd five-a-side game, but not many. I never saw him play professionally, but I think he knew his limits, and training with the likes of Mark Walters, Mark Hateley and Mo Johnston, that was probably best done from afar and with his trusty whistle. He did come on occasionally, but mainly to leave a wee reminder on cocky strikers like myself.

Training was a pleasure, laughter never far from our throats, and Walter revelled in the camaraderie that he had helped to form. Get the work done, that was a given, put the hard slog in, but being around us players, revelling in each other's company; you could see he loved it.

Not that he understood much of our more youthful ways. Walter was mad about music, but for ages, he couldn't get on with the stuff I liked. My punk bands, AC/DC, it wasn't his thing. 'Just noise,' he'd tell me. Walter was a man of the 1960s, loved everything about it, and to him, music ended with the Beatles. It was all about the Fab Four, and I tried to convince him that as great as the Beatles were, other stuff and other eras were worth a try.

He did get into Bon Jovi, and we went along together to see them and had a magic night. We also had a great night at Hampden when he joined me for the AC/DC gig. I was his assistant at Rangers at the time. He was reticent at first but, as the night went on, I glanced to my right and noticed an enthusiastic air-guitar coming from my companion, and a big grin forming across his face, as 'Let There Be Rock' was pelted up high into the Glaswegian sky.

At work, with Walter working under Graeme Souness, it was never really a case of 'Good Cop, Bad Cop'. Walter was always approachable, but had no time for being the shoulder to cry on. Graeme would make decisions that sometimes wound me up, decisions that I didn't always agree with. I could take that frustration to Walter. He would listen, nod, and then tell me why Graeme was right and how that particular decision was for the benefit of the team. That was that. The problem was no longer a problem. See you later.

Walter could look at us players and know if we were upset; he understood things about our particular personalities. Some managers put everyone in the same box. They are footballers. Simple as that. Treat them all the same. Walter went further. He knew each of his players and their individual characteristics, and because of that he could get the best out of them.

He watched me play and knew very quickly that I was torn between being an out-and-out goalscorer and a deeper-lying forward, able to link the play. It preyed on my mind at times and Walter was able to pull me to one side, saying that he understood my thought process and sometimes I wanted to be more involved in the build-up play, but it could not be to the detriment of my goalscoring and therefore the team. He talked me through it and with that I focused on being more advanced, and more goals came my way. Simple but very effective.

When Graeme went to the Rangers chairman, David Murray, in the spring of 1991, and said he had made his mind up and would take the Liverpool job, Murray asked when he might leave. 'At the end of the season,' was Graeme's considered response. We were still in a title race after all, but Murray had other ideas. He told him, 'You can go now.' David was a shrewd man and he said that to Graeme because he knew he had a seamless replacement in Walter Smith.

Walter was offered the job and I remember going for a shower. Walter was in there. I knew what was going on behind the scenes, and after a bit I said, 'What are you thinking?'

'What do you think?' he said.

'You gotta take it.'

'Aye, you're right.'

That was it.

Having won us the league that May with a depleted team (the club's fourth in a row), he took the unbelievable work done by Graeme and built on it, turning the club into what I believe was, at the time, by far the best team in Britain.

In 1993, he took us very close to a Champions League final, the first under the competition's new format. We were competing with and beating the best, and I know Walter loved every minute of it. Not only watching us players have so many incredible experiences, but because it gave him the chance to flex his tactical muscles on the biggest stage of all.

At home, people like Sir Alex Ferguson were clearly big fans of his. Having already used his talents with the national team, Fergie would later appoint Walter as his assistant at Manchester United. Further afield, similarly esteemed coaches such as Marcello Lippi were very much in awe of him, and the two became great friends with a lovely respect between them. To see them in the same room was like looking at twins!

If back-to-back Scottish titles and Europe's premium club competition didn't satiate his desire to win, Walter would take his competitiveness out on those of us who would play golf with him, or who took part in the many regular quiz nights that he so adored. He loved his music, his sport and his general knowledge. What he didn't like was losing. We'd always seem to end up on separate sides, and even when the girls joined us, there would be hell if things weren't going well. I was probably just as bad to be honest, and whilst these evenings were supposed to be fun, I'm not sure either he or I were really having any.

And it wasn't just me that Walter hated losing to. Even the most revered of our football nobility could turn his competitive switch up to full blast.

One day, we're playing golf on a course near Manchester in 2008. Sir Alex and myself make up one pair, and Walter is in the other, with big Jimmy Stewart, Rangers' goalkeeping coach. Fergie puts his tee shot up to the right into the trees. Walter hits his up to the left on the fairway.

So, we're away in the buggy and Fergie is in these trees, having a look for his ball. After a while, Fergie is shouting, 'I've found it, I've got it!'

I'm nearby and then, coming from the trees, a quieter voice. It's Fergie again. 'Alistair . . . Alistair.'

'What is it?' I ask.

'Is tha' bastar' lookin'?'

'What?'

'Tha' bastar'. Is he lookin'?'

Before I can answer, from a golf buggy some one hundred yards away, comes Walter's voice. 'Aye, I'm fuckin' lookin'!'

Walter could mix with, and in some cases shout at the best, because he was amongst the best. He was cut from the same cloth as all our great Scottish managers, and like them, his qualities were simple, effective and demanded respect. Walter reminded me of my dad; they got on and understood each other. He certainly became more and more like a father to me, after my own died in the summer of 1994. It was an incredibly difficult time. Dad and my Uncle George had both passed away within weeks of each other, and then Davie Cooper left us in the March of 1995. On each occasion, Walter was the first to offer his support.

However, he also reminded me of my lovely wee mum. Like her, Walter took great pleasure in seeing those around him having a good time. It's a rare and wonderful trait, and they both had it. They would take a selfless delight in seeing happiness. My mum loved nothing more than having people over, listening to us all tell our stories and laughing, whilst she brewed the tea and warmed the morning rolls. With Walter, you knew that if his staff and his players were happy, as long as their work was getting done, so was he.

Not that he liked to let on if he found your joke funny. That would be too easy, but there were times when he cracked. One occasion came when I was desperately trying to make our Algerian midfielder, Brahim Hemdani, laugh. A great lad, Brahim, but the big man was not prone to a smile. Nothing could change his stern impression. It wouldn't do.

'I don't care if takes me two months or eighteen, I am going to make the boy laugh,' I said confidently.

Walter assessed the situation and said, 'You've nae chance . . .'

Challenge accepted. Three months later and I have thrown all my best material at him, but there's not a whiff of even a snigger.

'Any joy gettin' that bastard to smile yet?' Walter asked.

'No, nae chance,' I replied. 'I think you might be right.'

But then an opportunity arose. My last chance.

We were in the coaches' room at Murray Park. It was downstairs. There were some toilets in one room with the showers, and some lockers for our stuff, but there was also a door that didn't go anywhere. You'd open it and there was just a bricked wall above a small storage unit.

'This is the last throw of the fuckin' dice,' I told the gaffer.

We finish training one day and I say to Hemdani, you need to come in, the gaffer wants a word. 'Come in about ten or fifteen minutes.'

I let Durranty and our coach, Kenny McDowall, in on the gag, and they are in the coaches' room with me. There's a knock on the door. 'Come in . . .'

It's Hemdani. He looks at me, with that serious expression of his.

I let him stand there for five minutes, pretending to be on the phone. 'Alright, gaffer . . . nice one, gaffer . . . yes, gaffer . . . I'll send him right in, gaffer.'

He's looking at me still, so I put the phone on the desk, point to the phantom door, and I say, 'He's through there, big man, on you go.'

Hemdani walks towards the door, opens it, and is stood there in front of the brick wall. Now I am in bits. Durranty and Kenny too. We're on the floor laughing. Hemdani looks the wall up and down, turns around, sees us in bits, walks by us, and leaves the room without the merest of smirks. I had failed and would never try anything again. When I went up the stairs to tell Walter, I thought he was going to have a heart attack from laughing.

The other time Walter showed off his magical sense of humour was the time I stitched our goalkeeping coach at Jimmy Stewart right up. It was a Friday, the meeting on the day before the game, and without fail Walter had to have an Empire biscuit. For those uneducated in Scottish biscuits, these are two shortbread biscuits with a jam filling, icing on top and decorated with a jelly sweet. The real deal, and Walter insisted that there would be one at his seat in the meeting room, and no one else need look at it.

The meeting is at 2 p.m. I'm downstairs and Walter says to me, 'The meeting is at quarter past two, I'm running late.'

'Nae bother, gaffer,' I say. 'I'll tell the boys.'

I go upstairs, the tea's laid out, the cakes are there and so is the gaffer's Empire biscuit. I'd said to Durranty to phone me at ten past two and not to say anything. We're sitting there, my phone goes, it's Durranty and, like I've asked, he's saying nothing. I begin to talk. 'All right, gaffer . . . that's not a problem, gaffer . . . see you then,' and I put the phone down.

Big Jimmy Stewart is sat there. 'Wha's that all about?' he asks.

'It's the gaffer, he's not making the meeting, something's come up. He's headed to Glasgow and he'll see us at the ground tomorrow.'

'Nae bother.'

Thirty seconds later, Big Jimmy cracks. His big goalkeeping hand is across the table, and he's in. He's gone for the big one. He's gone for the Empire biscuit.

'He willnae be needing that, then.'

I am watching it unfold in slow motion. The top teeth are just hitting the icing, the bottom gnashers are driving into the shortbread, the door opens and it's the gaffer. I'm up, and we're pointing and shouting, 'Hey, gaffer, what about the big yin eating your Empire biscuit?!'

I can safely say that Jimmy has never eaten one since. For Walter, the disgust on his face soon turned to a knowing smile and that quiet but bouncing laugh of his, as it dawned on him that we had royally, or empirically, stitched up our pal.

Walter sometimes had to have a sense of humour. After all, for three years he managed Paul Gascoigne. Gazza was like a force of nature at Ibrox, and I believe he found the perfect manager in Walter. A man who understood him (as much as anyone can understand Gazza), knew when to be compassionate and when not to be. Gazza responded to Walter like no other manager, who I think got the best from him.

The first time Walter ever met Gascoigne was on holiday. Gazza was in a hotel swimming pool, playing with Walter's fabulous sons Neil and Steven. Walter watched them all splashing about, thinking how great Gazza was with kids, but every now and then, Gazza would shout out, 'PCDS!' Walter kept hearing this shout from him. Every twenty minutes or so, there it was again. 'PCDS!' Walter looked away to chat, and then heard it again. Two weeks later, Walter found out that 'PCDS!' was a shout to the hotel bar staff and meant, 'Piña Colada, Double Strength!'

Gazza would have us all in hysterics, Walter too, although I think he could drive him insane. I was a breath of fresh air to Walter compared to Gascoigne, but the gaffer knew there was a tender side to the player and how he should be looked after. Gazza would receive and accept invites to Walter's for Christmas lunch, and that kindness was typical of Walter.

He cared about all the people at the club and it wasn't just about management or because it might help the bottom line, results. No, Walter was born with a warmth and an understanding that was perfect when it came to looking after someone like Paul Gascoigne.

If you asked Gazza, I am pretty certain that he would say that the two most influential men in his footballing career were Terry Venables and Walter Smith. It was all about getting the best from Gazza, nurturing him, but also knowing that he was not there to be micro-managed.

Walter told a story about being in Glasgow one day, shortly after Gazza's arrival. He bumped into Billy Connolly in a shop and the two guys were having a chat, when the player's name came up. 'How's Gazza, Walter?' the Big Yin asked.

'Oh, Gazza is Gazza,' Walter replied. 'He's keeping us on our toes, but he's a great guy, and what a footballer.'

Billy then gave him some advice. 'Remember, you have to live with the genius, the genius will not live with you.'

That stayed with Walter, who never forgot that Gazza was not there to be changed or somehow moulded to suit him and the club. He was there and you just had to enjoy the man, however crazy it might get. Yes, you could give him a clip around the ear when he needed one, but his madness was part of that genius.

Walter was always great with me, although people will tell you that the genius bit was never an issue. There were plenty of things he did for me that helped to make me a better footballer, but it was the faith he showed in me as a player and a man that stays with me. Like my own parents, Walter believed in me. I'll never forget the day in 1992 when he came to me in the hotel, one evening before a game at Dundee United. I was sat with the boys and in walked Walter, who looked my way and gave me the eyes. He wanted a word.

As I walked out the door, I was thinking, I don't believe it, the bastard is dropping me.

'Listen,' he said. Here we go. 'Listen, Goughie's injured for a couple of months. I'm making you captain.'

My jaw dropped. To be made captain of the club I supported as a boy, that was up there with any great moment in my career, and it blew my mind for Walter to see something in me, his centre forward, worth giving me the responsibility. I'll never forget walking the team out, with the armband on, and feeling on top of the world. My teammates must have thought Walter had lost it. 'If that bastard can make captain, with his timekeeping, then there is hope for us all!'

The pride that I felt then, Walter gave to me again when he came to me in 2004 with an offer. I had been doing my media work for several years, and was enjoying being a team captain on *A Question of Sport*, when Walter called and asked me out for a pizza and a glass of wine. Halfway through, he told me he had the Scotland job and asked if I would like to come along and help him.

Now, it was Walter who had firmly encouraged me and Durranty to get our coaching badges. Like a father telling his sons to get a paper round, Walter was adamant that it was for our own good, and with his goading we both got them all, right up to UEFA Pro Licence.

With those qualifications, I presumed Walter was asking me to help with the Under-16s or other kids' groups. That would have been great, but when he told me he wanted me to be one of his assistants with the seniors, I was flabbergasted. Where did I sign?

Walter, in his wonderful way, told me to think about it. He said to go away for a week, that I had great media work, stuff I could still do, but that I was good at it, I could have a career at it, and I shouldn't rush into any decision that I might later regret. Typical Walter. Always thinking of others. Suffice to say that a week later, I emphatically said yes.

Walter was so clever. With me agreeing to jump on board, he also got Tommy Burns in, and the three of us had the times of our lives. The late Tam was one of the greatest men anyone has ever met. I loved him. The only man to make me look punctual, and we bounced not only jokes off each other, but footballing ideas too. With Walter at the helm, the nation was galvanised after quite a few years in the doldrums. I'd like to think the players enjoyed that spell with the national team and results suggested so, because Walter got the country seventy or so places up the FIFA rankings.

Not that I think Walter was always 100 per cent convinced he had done the right thing getting me and Tam together. We had a training session in Milan prior to a game against Italy. Walter came to me and Tam, and said, 'You guys go ahead to the San Siro. I've got you a car. Get everything set up there, on the pitch, so we're ready to crack on when I arrive with the players.'

'Nae bother, gaffer,' we both said.

So, Tam and I were in this cab and it took us through the centre of Milan and into big traffic. We were stuck there and it was clear we were going to be very late. When we finally arrived at the stadium, we got out the car and saw through some fences that there were players training in the distance. Tam squinted to get a closer look, saw blue jerseys and a smile spread across his face.

'The Italians are training,' he said. 'We're early. We can get in there and have a good look at the oppo. Walter will be so pleased with us.'

I stepped in to have a look, covered my eyes to shade out the sun, and turned to Tam. 'I have some bad news, mate,' I said. 'That's our lot out there. We're late. Very late.'

We strolled out onto the pitch with a bag of bibs and some balls, and the players already working away. When Walter saw us, we just got a shake of the head, that disappointed look all paternal figures can give to make their kids feel about two inches tall.

If we felt stupid that day in Milan, the nation enjoyed some joyful nights under Walter, none more so than the 1–0 victory over France at Hampden in 2006. The place was jumping when Gary Caldwell scored a winner, and it showed all of

Walter's abilities as a coach and manager because, make no mistake, France, with Thierry Henry, Lilian Thuram, Patrick Vieira, Franck Ribéry and Claude Makélélé, were right up there with the best in the world. After the game, I said to Walter, 'That might just be your best ever result in football.' He simply smiled and took a sip of his wine.

Working alongside Walter, I learnt more and more about the man. I was learning every day on the training pitch with him, but watching him closely as his assistant, I got a feel for the real class of the man. Small things like noticing he would always present the opposing national team's manager or coach with a beautiful bottle of whisky in a case. It had nothing to do with the Scottish FA, it wasn't a gimmick, but Walter organised it himself. He bought the bottle and it was just something he wanted to do. It was as if he was so proud of the country and its products, he wanted to show it off in the form of a gift. Class act.

To work with Walter and to enjoy nights like the France victory, it was magic. Knowing what it meant to him, seeing how well he worked with the players and to reap some kind of reward from that, was everything. So, when Rangers came knocking in 2007 and Walter asked me to join him; well, I was never going to say no.

Once again, we had some great times at club level and Walter built a team capable of competing with the best. I remember a game in the Champions League against Frank Rijkaard's Barcelona in 2007. They were some team and the greats who would play under Pep Guardiola were there: Andrés Iniesta, Xavi, Lionel Messi was coming through. Then there was the likes of Ronaldinho and Henry in amongst them too. They came to Ibrox and Walter had the lads organised and committed, and we kept it goalless. I'll never forget, right at the end of the match they had the ball, but Rijkaard was gesturing to his team to keep it, and to see out the time. 'We'll take the draw.'

Rangers made it to the final of the UEFA Cup that season, a special achievement and one that meant so much to Walter. Not that he always kept right up with affairs. We played Fiorentina for the semi-final in Florence that went to penalties. Walter would not get involved in picking the penalty takers. 'You do it,' he'd say to me and Kenny McDowall. When he asked later who was taking them, I gave him the five.

We missed our first but then started scoring, and Fiorentina, including seasoned internationals like Christian Vieri, missed a couple. Nacho Novo, our Spanish forward, began his walk to the spot.

Walter turned to me and said, 'What's the score?'

I thought he was winding me up and smiled nervously.

'I'm nae kidding, what's the score?'

'I'll tell you now,' I said, 'if wee Nacho scores this penalty, you're about to find out the score.'

Nacho did score, and Walter and I were in an embrace that seemed to go on for hours. That's what I miss, that sense of shared joy that simply being with Walter could bring on. Two men, two friends, clinging on to each other in a moment of sheer, unadulterated delight.

That joy turned to deep concern, when some years later, Walter sat me down for a chat and told me he had cancer. As usual, he was worried about the people he was telling, remaining upbeat and keeping that sense of humour, and as the months passed – with the operation seemingly a success – we hoped that he had rid himself of it. But the cancer came back, and in the autumn of 2021, we received the news that he had died.

I was working at talkSPORT, doing the breakfast show, when I saw I had a missed call from Steven, Walter's son. I knew what was coming. I'd been to the hospital and at the house to see him, and so knowing how unwell he was, I took myself away to make the call back. Silence. It is hard to know what to say, but knowing just how much Walter adored his wife Ethel, his kids and his grandkids, and the severe grief they were now going through, my thoughts were immediately with them. Neil and Steven are two chips off the old block, the best company like their father, and I am so pleased to call the whole family friends.

In the spring of 2024, Rangers unveiled a statue of Walter Smith. It depicts the man beautifully, and is the perfect tribute to all that he gave to the club and to the game. It stands on the corner of the Copland Road stand, a spot that Walter first strolled along with his grandad Jock to see the club they loved, and one that he would serve so well.

Walter served the whole country in so many different ways, and all the achievements, the titles and the medals that he accumulated will always be there to remind us of what he did. They are not what really matter, though. Not in the long run. At Walter's memorial service, I was honoured to be asked to say a few words. In conclusion, I quoted the great American poet and activist, Maya Angelou, who wrote, 'People will forget what you said, people will

forget what you did, but people will never forget how you
made them feel.'

Today, I can think about my friend and whilst the pain of
not having him with us remains, it subsides as I close my eyes
and think of everything he was to me in my life. I can think
of Walter and I can remember how he made me feel. Special.

eleven

LIGHTING THE FIREWORKS

HERE's a name for you. Alexander Watson Hutton. You may not have heard of him, but to some of us Scots, he remains one of the most integral figures in the long history of Scottish football. Did he win many international caps? Not one. Score many league goals? None. Did he manage early Scottish league clubs? Nope.

Watson Hutton was born in the Gorbals area of Glasgow in 1853, becoming a sports-mad schoolteacher who emigrated to Argentina in 1882. By now football had taken off in Britain with gusto, but it was in his new home that he spread the word. In the schools that he founded in Buenos Aires, the game began to blossom with a South American feel, and under the Glasgow man's stewardship, the Argentine Association Football League was created in 1893. It was the first football league outside of the British Isles, and with Watson Hutton's help and the game's growing popularity, a football association was born, the national team began to excel, and eventually three World Cups were won.

Today, Watson Hutton is buried in Buenos Aires and the library at the Argentine Football Association is named after him. Ask those in the know out there, and they will gladly call the schoolteacher from the Gorbals 'the father of Argentine football'. Why am I going on about Alexander Watson Hutton? Well, the way I see it, if it wasn't for Watson Hutton, there may well not have been a Diego Maradona, and therefore us Scots can (and do) sit back, sip on a wee dram, and take a fair share of the credit for not only one of the greatest players the world has ever seen, but his two goals that knocked England out of the 1986 World Cup.

Clutching at straws? Too right I am, but when it comes to football's oldest rivalry, any Scottish foot on an English throat must be taken with undiluted joy. However tenuous it may be. If you walk into a pub in Scotland, you will find in many of them, pinned up on a bit of wall behind the bar, a grainy photograph of Maradona in his now infamous 'Hand of God' pose.

It is there to celebrate a moment of English demise, but because of our Glaswegian ancestor – who brought the game to the very streets of Buenos Aires that gave the world Maradona – Scotland's part in it must also be celebrated. The English might find that petty, and they may be right, but schadenfreude is best when it wears tartan.

I can't put my finger on the precise moment that I understood the age-old rivalry between the football teams of Scotland and England. I do know that one of my very earliest footballing memories was watching the 1970 World Cup in

Mexico. I wasn't yet eight years old, but the football on our new colour television was enthralling, as was the quarter-final between Sir Alf Ramsey's England and West Germany.

England were 2-0 up with about twenty minutes to go, but after Beckenbauer scored to make it 2-1, Bobby Charlton was taken off, presumably to rest his legs for a possible semi-final. Despite being replaced with a quality player in Colin Bell, the Germans then took control. They levelled things 2–2 and then in extra time, Gerd Müller, a player who would soon become an idol of mine, scored an acrobatic volley from close range past Peter Bonetti, and England were out.

I was watching with my mum and dad. Scotland didn't make World Cups then. The thought was fanciful, and whilst there was no wild celebrating at our poor neighbours' demise, I can safely say that no one in the McCoist household fell into a bout of depression either. It was just quietly there. My dad and his friends, all football crazy, were subtly smiling for a couple of days. I didn't ask, but looking back, I can imagine why. For four years they had lived with the consistent reminders from down south of their world champion status. Four more years and it might have got a bit boring.

I was certainly too young to acknowledge any historical rivalry. Over a drink, my dad and those friends would crow about that legendary team they called the Wembley Wizards, the 1928 side who went to Wembley and won 5–1, a highlight still to many of us Scots who have taken a keen interest in the world's oldest international football fixture.

Scotland vs England. The first ever international game was played in 1872 at the West of Scotland Cricket Club in the Partick area of Glasgow, a ground that still stands there today, and one where Rangers used to train often in my days at the club. We would all get on the minibus and head over there, some of us appreciating the history of the place and the match that gave birth to international football.

It is said that football in Scotland goes back much further than that, often with macabre connotations. In the border town of Jedburgh, they still play the frantic game of Hand Ba', an old medieval version of the beautiful game, before it got its makeover. It's basically a mob version of football with locals chasing a ball around, attempting to get it into goals on the opposite side of town. It remains a tradition, but fortunately, the fact that when it started the ball used was the head of some poor dead English soldier, has been largely neglected.

When the English arrived in Glasgow in November 1872, their heads were firmly on their shoulders, but worryingly those shoulders were very broad. Football in Victorian England was a game for the elite. The players were sons of the aristocracy, old Etonians, well-bred and well-fed, wearing top hats and cravats; I can imagine the visitors must have fancied their chances on seeing their smaller opponents, a Scottish winter having made them pale and weathered.

Football was very much a physical game to the English. Like the Empire, the new sport, and the FA rule book written at their universities, was all about gaining territory and that meant individually dribbling the ball upfield using strength and attrition. The Scots weren't really built for that, and whilst they managed to keep the English at bay for a goalless draw in that first international game, in time Scotland's tactics became all about teamwork rather than celebrating the lone individual.

The passing game, as we now know it, was born and with these idiosyncrasies, the Scots began to dominate the fixture. Of the first sixteen games, us Scots won ten, including a 7–2 win at the original Hampden Park in 1878 and a 6–1 win in London at the Kennington Oval.

With such obvious skill and knowhow, it wasn't long before the new English Football League clubs sought to tap into our clear knowledge and superiority, bringing plenty of us Scots down with offers of work and relative wealth, in the hope that their success could rub off on them. It worked and the English clubs blossomed. Those Scottish pioneers were known as the Scotch Professors, and they benefited most of the northern powerhouses in the game: Blackburn Rovers, Sunderland and Preston North End all won honours thanks to their new Scottish employees. Liverpool's first ever XI in 1892 was made up completely of Scots.

Despite so many of us making the move south, the game in Scotland didn't cease in its own expansion and popularity and by 1892, Glasgow housed all three of the biggest football stadiums (Ibrox, Celtic Park and the new Hampden) on the entire planet. Say it quietly, but it's as if Scotland is indeed the real home of football, isn't it?

Now, if I had my way, this chapter would finish here. A nice clean ending with the nation sitting firmly on top of football's new and ever blossoming tree. But unfortunately time moves on, and whilst we continued to enjoy great moments such as those Wizards casting their witchcraft at Wembley in 1928, I have to report that England improved and every now and then gave us the odd beating too.

One such occasion was at Wembley in 1961. With the post-war fixtures becoming more and more tribal, England were glad to be at home. The late, great Jimmy Armfield used to joke that the England team would drive through Glasgow on the way to Hampden, the streets would be lined with the locals, nine or ten deep, and that 'all were eager to show us their wedding rings'.

The Scots boasted plenty of legendary names that day at Wembley. Billy McNeil, Dave Mackay, Denis Law, Ian St John, Eric Caldow – not too shabby. Eric was a wonderful guy, whom I got to know at Rangers. He'd played over 250 games for the club, won forty caps for Scotland, fifteen as captain, and was one of those old-school footballing gentlemen. He would be at Ibrox for every game, the blazer and the club tie on, hair immaculate, always there with a smile and up for a chat. I felt a reverence towards men like Eric.

Bob McPhail was another one. An Ibrox legend, a forward who held the club's post-war goalscoring record, and as I started to edge nearer to it, he was always there to greet me, again in the blazer and tie. 'Won't be long now, Alistair,' he used to say to me.

'Not sure about that, Mr McPhail,' I'd say, as if greeting a headteacher.

When I did break his 57-year-old record against Raith Rovers in 1996, the first man to meet me in the tunnel was Bob, and with a smile and a handshake, he made my day. 'Congratulations, Alistair!' What a man.

Unfortunately for the tens of thousands of Scots who made their way to Wembley that afternoon, even the many great names of our game couldn't stem the flow of a fine English team that included Armfield, Johnny Haynes, Bobby Charlton, Bobby Smith and Jimmy Greaves. The latter two grabbing a brace and a hat-trick respectively.

The English like to brag about the game, the biggest winning margin in the fixture's history, but if you take a closer look, with fifteen minutes left it was only 5–3 to the hosts, before a collapse that saw four goals in seven minutes, adding to the sore heads that some of the visitors surely experienced the following morning.

In goal for Scotland that day, and nursing his own sore ego, was Celtic's Frank Haffey. It was his second and last game for the national team, and whilst many of the nine goals were far from his fault, some did squeeze through him or under him. That night on the way home, when an English newspaper photographer tricked him into posing next to platform 9 at King's Cross station, his humiliation was complete. Haffey emigrated to Australia soon after, but some older Scots still wonder if it was by choice.

With his three goals in the rout, Jimmy Greaves certainly took advantage of Haffey's bad day at the office, and years later he would make a television career shine with a constant jibe about Scottish goalkeeping and the quality (or lack of it) on show. Haffey's stint in goal that day must have got his mind ticking, and the likes of Alan Rough and Jim Leighton were unlucky to be on the end of his devilment.

Plenty of Scottish folk took umbrage at Greavsie's comments about our custodians, but that would only encourage the former England man. You have to laugh, and such was the humour and the cheeky patter with which Greavsie made his jokes, I think most of us would have secretly had him as a Scot, given the chance.

Five years after the 9–3 result, Jimmy cut a sad figure as he left the Wembley turf, an injury having stopped him from playing in England's World Cup final triumph. Some of the more nationalistic of us Scots would have argued that whatever misery he was feeling that day, they could see it and raise it by a hundred.

I was far too young to remember England's big victory in 1966, and as a football man, I can certainly marvel at what a great achievement it was, but I do like to hear about the likes of Denis Law, who was asked where he had watched the match that saw his teammates Bobby Charlton and Nobby Stiles win football's biggest prize. He replied that he hadn't and instead he had taken himself for a round of golf. As he strolled into the 19th hole after the round, he was told England had won. Legend has it that he offered one word in response: 'Bastards.'

I can confirm that later in my own career, had Chris Woods and Terry Butcher (my Rangers teammates in 1990 and members of England's World Cup squad that year) made it past the Germans in the semi-final, I would have been on the phone to the great Denis Law and organising a round at Turnberry.

The game in 1966 is special, but in this age of goal-line technology and VAR, I do like to ask my English friends to take a closer look at Geoff Hurst's vital third goal, and with hands on their hearts tell me the ball crossed the line. Many of them point to the reaction of Roger Hunt, Hurst's strike partner, and say that as a goalscorer he would have nodded the rebound in had it not crossed the line. Instead he held his hands aloft and by doing so conned the linesman. It was an act of heroic skulduggery. Geoff Hurst got the knighthood, but I reckon the Queen's sword should have been tapping Sir Roger's shoulders too.

Even recently I had some fun with that moment. It was at the 2022 World Cup final in Qatar when I was on co-comms. Sam Matterface was the commentator and myself and Lee Dixon were alongside him. When Kylian Mbappé scored his third goal late into extra time to take the game to penalties, the crowd were going mad and Sam was making his points. I then piped up with, 'What a special moment that is. Mbappé is the first person to score a hat-trick in a World Cup final . . .'

There was a pause, Lee went to turn to me, Sam pulled the microphone up to put me right, but before either could speak, I continued, '. . . where all three crossed the line.' The three of us all sat back, our shoulders bouncing up and down in silent laughter, unable to say anything for ten or so seconds. Social media wasn't that keen on me that night.

Sixty years on from 1966, and you can't begrudge the English for still going on about their win. In fact, if I have one annoyance, it would be that they don't go on about it enough, because I can tell them this. If or when Scotland win the World Cup, there will be massive banners and uplighting at St Andrew's, there will be 24-hour fireworks shooting up from a now blue-and-white Forth Bridge, and the M8 will be lined with those of us able and sober enough to do a Highland jig. And, by law, all of that will go on indefinitely.

I mean, we already have some form for such crowing, and that was when we became the world's 'unofficial' champions in April 1967, less than a year after England's somewhat fortunate victory over the West Germans. Scotland came to Wembley needing a win to secure that summer's Home Championship, but more importantly, knowing that victory would mean global bragging rights.

They came meaning business. A fact noticed immediately by Nobby Stiles when he saw that his Manchester United teammate, Denis Law – usually a player known for having his socks loosely around his ankles – was wearing shin-pads. Yes, this was far from a friendly.

Scotland might have been without wee Jimmy Johnstone and Bobby Murdoch, who just a few weeks later would help Celtic to Britain's first European Cup, but in the likes of Law, Jim Baxter, Billy Bremner, Tammy Gemmell and John Greig, they had players and proud Scots eager to take the wind from England's glorious sails.

And that is exactly what they did. Goals from Law and Bobby Lennox gave us a 2–0 lead, before Jack Charlton pulled one back, but a late goal from Sheffield Wednesday's Jim McCalliog restored a two-goal advantage that even a very late Hurst effort couldn't bridge.

No offence to McCalliog, but the greatest part of his goal, the match and possibly the history of Scottish football was in the build-up, when Jim Baxter slowed the game down to a trotting pace, flicked the ball up and started to do keepy-ups before laying the ball off. All under the nose of a snarling Nobby Stiles. The great Jim Baxter, very brilliant and very brave. Archie Macpherson later described Jim's moment of cheeky finesse as coming with an 'element of mischief'. I think what Archie meant to say was that Jim was taking the absolute piss.

It was a moment and a match that my dad and his pals never, ever tired of talking about. A lull in any conversation could be filled by a retelling of someone's version of the day Jim Baxter toyed with the English and the team became the champions of the world. As my love of football grew and grew, I also never tired of hearing about it.

My first real experience of our rivalry was a friendly in 1973 in a game marking the centenary of the Scottish FA, which England won 5–0. I wasn't at the match but as a ten-year-old, I recall thinking how downright rude the English were, given that we had invited them to our party and they had the temerity to give us a battering.

I seem to remember Leeds' Allan Clarke doing most of the damage, and Emlyn Hughes making one of his early appearances for England. Years later I would be on *A Question of Sport* with Emlyn and it's hard to tell what gave the great man more pleasure, the win itself, or telling me about it some fifteen years later.

The first game that I went to between the two countries was in May 1974, just before that summer's World Cup, and this time we won 2–0. Big Joe Jordan claimed the first, but it might have been an own goal from Stoke City's Mike Pejic, and then the second was a Colin Todd own goal following a shot from Kenny Dalglish. It was a great occasion, fuelled by the expectation of the upcoming World Cup in Germany, but it also gave me my first taste of a Hampden crowd playing against the auld enemy.

I could tell that this game was different. There was something more intense about the people there, a unity. Basically, this was some 90,000 Scots sharing one mutual goal, to send them back down the A74 with their tails between their legs. I was hooked.

And what a time to be hooked. Being a teenager in Scotland in the late 1970s was a joy, supporting the national team passionately and looking for bragging rights over those poor souls south of Carlisle. Not only were we planning for World Cups, whilst the English were only planning for Benidorm, we enjoyed an abundance of victories, at home and at their place.

In 1976, the wonderful Ray Clemence let in an effort through his legs from his soon-to-be teammate, Kenny Dalglish, and gifted us not only the win, but the Home Championship; and not only the championship, but smiles as broad as Kenny's in the knowledge that an Englishman's misfortune had led to our delight.

Then in 1977, Jubilee year, another Kenny goal led to more jubilation, this time at Wembley, and a somewhat raucous celebration from the thousands of fans in the ground, in England's capital and partying at home. With England failing to get to either the 1974 or 1978 World Cups, it truly did feel like we were kings of our island. And oh, how we let them know it.

When I became a professional footballer, a common route for players in Scotland was to go south, and whilst I never felt a great pull to be an English First Division footballer, when the opportunity arose to move to Sunderland, it was one that excited me. Not because I felt that the English game was superior, but I wanted to step up a level, and seeing some of the players I'd be sharing a dressing room with at Roker Park, I felt it was a place I could continue to learn. And learn I did.

Sunderland is a great club, with a loyal following. Passionate like you wouldn't believe. We had a good squad and the manager, Alan Durban, was an energetic Welshman building a young team that included myself, Colin West, Nick Pickering and Barry Venison, though maybe we were too young, because the first season was a struggle in England.

I wasn't scoring anywhere near the amount of goals the club or myself had hoped, but I was learning. We avoided relegation on the last game of the season with a 1–0 victory over Manchester City, and immediately flew as a squad to celebrate in Majorca. It was there that I met one of the great English talents and characters, Frank Worthington, who had recently signed for us.

Not only did I meet Frank, but I was asked to room with him. There are some that might think that putting an impressionable nineteen-year-old footballer into a room with Frank Worthington might be a mistake, and if there was anything such as an HR department in those days, they should have been quickly notified. But truth be told, being with Frank was one of the great things that happened to me as a young pro.

First of all, what a footballer he was. Frank was coming to the end of his glittering career, but the things he could do in training and on match day, they took your breath away. He played like he lived, with a freedom, and to be with him, to listen to his advice and laugh at his stories, highlighted everything I wanted from the game.

He loved his football. Yes, there were the hairstyles, the jewellery, the champagne and the odd girlfriend, but Frank was happiest with the ball at his feet, under his spell. He looked so at ease and at home with it. Some say the great players are on first-name terms with the football. Frank was its best pal, golfing partner and the best man at its wedding.

There would be nights out, but they were just as educational as the football, and the thing was with Frank, no matter what we did the night before, he was there at 9 a.m. Without fail, he would have a cup of tea and some toast, and then he'd be out there, working.

Even when we went abroad, during close season, Frank was up, tea and toast ready, and then he'd get me out to the tennis court, and let me tell you, Frank was as enthusiastic and competitive about tennis as he was about football and a good night out. The tennis whites, the Bjorn Borg headbands and wristbands, always looking and playing the part. What a guy. I loved him.

My time in England was short, but I saw it as another part of my apprenticeship, not only in the ways of being a footballer, but in dealing with the English. I'd need those lessons, because four years after I signed for Rangers back home, I had several of them sharing my dressing room. Two of the first to arrive, Chris Woods and Terry Butcher, played against me in my first game for Scotland against England.

In fact, on that day in May 1987, England had more Rangers players than Scotland. The game finished goalless, without much action, unlike those regular Scotland vs England five-a-sides we played at Rangers. Not much love was lost on those occasions, and if Graeme Souness was looking to prick the team's competitive streak, he certainly succeeded.

I have to say, it was absolute magic to have them all playing with us. Every single Englishman who came up added to the squad. Take Ray Wilkins, possibly the nicest man of all time, and one who enjoyed the most sterling career in England, Scotland and abroad. Before his tragic death, Ray stated that he felt his time at Rangers was the most fun and the most memorable. That says an awful lot for the environment that Graeme and Walter created, and for the good times we had with him.

I don't want to speak for any of them, but I think all of the English guys took to their new home. They embraced the country, from the square sausage and tattie scones on their new breakfast plates, to the beautiful homes they set up with their families. I don't think one of them would say they didn't enjoy playing up here. Some of the players like Kevin Drinkell stayed, some had their children born here, and whenever we get together, the old jokes and the old times come flooding back.

One of the best of times was the 1992/93 season, when under Walter Smith, we progressed in the new Champions League and we faced the English champions, Leeds United, in what the press labelled 'The Battle of Britain'. A bit over the top perhaps, but the game was a big deal at the time, and for us Rangers boys, a real chance to test ourselves and prove that we were the best around.

The first leg was at Ibrox. It was decided that there would be no away fans, which is always a shame, but the atmosphere was still amongst the most electric I ever witnessed at the old place. Maybe I was admiring the sound a bit too much, because only minutes in, my oversight led to the

English side taking the lead. Albeit with the help from a Scot and an old pal.

From a corner, the ball popped out to the edge of the box, and rather than picking up the onrushing Gary McAllister, like I was supposed to do, I was ball-watching. I could only stand and admire the perfect volley from my old boys team-mate, which flew unerringly into the top corner. Gary of all people. What a strike, though.

As I trudged back to the halfway line, there was a tap on my backside. It was Gary Mac. 'What do you think of that for a wee strike, son?' he said. If I was raging, I later found out that one punter, a Rangers fan, had confidently put £40,000 on us to win that match. Not sure I was his favourite Ranger at that point.

However, things changed and, spurred on by the crowd, we forced John Lukic in their goal into an error to equalise and not long before halftime, I was able to make it 2–1. We were going to England with an advantage, and it was one that an Englishman, Mark Hateley, extended with an incredible half-volley early on at their place.

What a magic goal it was. A strike, like Gary Mac's at Ibrox, which deserved the roar of an away end, but it wasn't to be. Not that Rangers fans didn't get in. I remember the drive to Elland Road that night. Leeds fans were everywhere, of course, politely making hand gestures to tell us what they thought of us, and as we got closer to the ground, it was crazily busy, mayhem – banging on the bus, the works. They were giving us loads. Welcome to Yorkshire.

Just as we pulled up, amongst all the Leeds fanatics, I recognised a face, a great lad called Stewart Daniels, Rangers crazy. He was surrounded by bedlam. Stewie caught my eye, gave me a wry smile and undid his jacket to show me a glimpse of his Rangers top, then put his hand to his forehead and gave me a salute. In this pressure cooker of a place, the biggest of games about to unfold, I was doubled over with the sheer audacity of this Glaswegian guy, firmly in enemy territory, somehow giving us his support.

And he wasn't alone. When Mark scored his magnificent goal, I was sure I heard a fracas and it was another guy I knew, big Andy Smilie, arguably the biggest Rangers fan of them all. Big Andy had managed to wangle an executive box. He had a scaffolding company and he said that he was bringing a load of Leeds mates and employees to see the game. Instead he brought twenty Rangers fans and when Mark scored they went crazy; all you could hear were Leeds fans banging on the glass, and not because they were after new Scottish pen pals.

In the second half, Leeds were fighting to get back into the tie, but with our lot playing a brilliant European game of consolidation, we broke, and with Hateley marauding down the right, I peeled away from the centre-half and met his perfect cross with a solid header. I wheeled away knowing that was pretty much that.

A glorious feeling and one that brought on a gloat I could not deny myself. On the way back to the halfway line, having taken the love from my teammates, I found myself headed towards Gary Mac. I hadn't forgotten his tap on my arse at Ibrox, so, having given him one back and with the same wry smile on my face, I said, 'What do you think of that for a wee heider, then?'

For me it was a rare win over the English, and four years later I had to watch a teammate get the better of me. When Gazza scored his wonder goal for England against us Scots at Wembley in the Euro '96 championships, I was unable to enjoy the sheer skill of the man, but when it comes to my relationship with England and its people, I will always cherish the time I worked with Paul Gascoigne and the enduring friendship that still exists today.

Gazza came to us in 1995. Walter had headed to Rome and literally doorstepped him, asking him to come from Lazio. The two very special men got on well together. Gazza fancied playing for him, and with Walter's perfect support and man management, I do believe that the Scottish game got the very best of him as a footballer.

He took to us as much as we took to him, and whilst we suddenly had to be on our toes every day at training, Gazza helped to make not only the team better, but our lives. That's how fun it was to be around him. Even on the many occasions when he would walk away from training in your clothes, leaving you with something of his, the whole dressing room would be close to hysterics.

There are so many stories, so many examples of Gazza's dedication to fun, and whilst we were all on the very sharp end of his antics at some point, recalling our time with him always brings a very big laugh. Even Gordon Durie would agree. I think.

Jukebox was on the end of one of Gazza's most notorious pranks, and I was lucky enough to get a ringside seat. Gazza came to Scotland and stayed in Kilbarchan, a Renfrewshire village. There he enjoyed the outdoor life, and as both a keen angler and insomniac, he would be found night or day by the water, fishing for the beautiful local trout.

Now, it was a long-held tradition at Rangers that players would come into training in a collar and tie. That was the rule and Gazza stuck to it, always punctual, maybe even early for training, but one day he was late and we began to wonder about him.

Suddenly, the door was flung open and there was Gazza in full fishing regalia, waders on up to his armpits, but underneath he was wearing a collar and tie. If that wasn't enough to bring the house down, in his hands were two of the biggest and plumpest trout you've ever seen in your life.

As it turned out, both Gazza and myself were injured that day, and so whilst the boys were away on the minibus to train, he and I had some treatment. Then he said, with that look of his, 'C'mon, Coisty, let's have a laugh with the fish.'

'Wha' d'ya mean?' I ask.

'Who's been annoying you?' he asks back.

I have a think about it, but I say, 'Jukebox. Gordon Durie has been really annoying me.'

'Right, get into his pockets and get his car keys.'

We go into his pockets and get the keys, unlock his car, and Gazza goes and fetches the trout.

I'm wondering what is going to happen, but Gazza gets into the boot where the spare wheel is kept and he throws in a fish. I go to throw the other fish in with it, but Gazza is having none of it. He takes the other trout, finds a secret little compartment in the backseats, one that no one would know existed, and he throws the other fish in there. With a smile on his face, Gazza turns to me and says, 'When he finds the first fish, he'll think that's it.' He walks away like a master criminal having pulled off the most perfect heist.

For the next three or four days, Jukebox was with us in training, complaining about the smell of his car. He moaned that people were walking by when he was stopped at traffic lights and putting their noses up at the stench coming from his motor.

Gordon looked in his boot, pulled the thing apart, and he found the first fish. He knew it was Gazza and he was effing and blinding, but he thought that's that. Problem solved. It wasn't though, was it? For another few days he came in, saying, 'For the life of me, I can't get rid of that smell.'

Gazza was trying hard not to laugh and I was the same, but neither of us could contain ourselves when one day we were strolling through the car park. We caught a look inside Gordon's car, and there were dozens and dozens of those tree-shaped car fresheners hanging everywhere. I swear, it looked like Sherwood Forest in there. It took the poor guy an age to discover the second fish and even then, another month to rid his wheels of the rotting stench, but even Jukebox couldn't stay angry with Gazza for long. No one could.

Another classic was the day I decided to put on a bit of a firework display for the kids. I am in the dressing room chatting to Durranty and Ian Ferguson about my plans, when over slides Gazza with an odd look in his eye, that suggests he has a secret to tell. Without looking at me, but from the side of his mouth, he says, 'By the way, I couldn't help but overhear your plans, Coisty.'

'Aye, what about them, Gazza?' I say.

'If it's fireworks you're after, I'm your man.'

Now at this point, any rational or vaguely sane human being would have stopped the conversation there. Gazza and fireworks are not the most compatible pairing, especially to anyone who hopes not to burn their house down, but when he tells me he can get £100 boxes for fifteen quid, the prudent side of me prone to a deal kicks in, and I ask to know more.

'Can you get me a couple?'

'Aye, no bother.'

I am told to meet Jimmy Five Bellies, his great mate, at the back of the Celtic End the next morning with the cash. Again, with Jimmy involved I should be running a mile, but the next morning there I am bright and early, and there is Jimmy in his Range Rover with tinted windows, waiting to make the drop. It looks like a drugs deal, but he's out of the car, the boot is opened, I give him the cash and I take the huge boxes, packaged in two big black bags.

We say our goodbyes and Jimmy is away in the car up the Copland Road, whilst I go training before going home to ready myself for what I hope is an adequate firework display. A few of my mates, Knoxy and others, are over, the kids are there and soon I think it's time to have a look at Gazza's rockets. When I say rockets, I should say Exocet missiles.

The first rocket has this head on it the size of a football. The next one up must have been manned. That's how big it is, and so we push its stem into the ground, get the kids safely back and toss a coin to see who lights it. I lose, so I approach it tentatively like some sort of Sellafield employee, light the thing, and quickly head back to watch as it flies up into the Bridge of Weir sky.

It keeps going and it keeps going for what seems like an age, and just as I am turning to Knoxy to say, 'Tha' bastar' has conned us here,' the entire village is lit up as it explodes into a cacophony of colours, shapes and sounds, like I have never seen from any firework before. The kids are in raptures, everyone is ecstatic, and we all agree that it is the best display anyone, anywhere has ever seen.

A few nights later, my missus and myself are coming home from a club dinner. I get into bed and she's washing her face, when the phone goes. She takes the call, and comes running up to the bedroom and says I have to get up! I have to get up because that was Gazza, who lives in the next village, and he wants to use one of those rockets he has left. He's going to point it in the direction of our village, to find out if we can see it.

I'm moaning about wanting my sleep. It's half two in the morning and I have training the next day, but before I can say another thing, our bedroom has lit up, and outside the whole village is iridescent with this explosion and I am falling on my bed, howling with laughter.

We go back to bed, but I can't sleep as I am still sniggering, when the phone goes again. This time it is the police. A serious-sounding sergeant, who tells me they have a Mr Gascoigne there, as they've had to pay him a visit after fireworks came from his property at this ungodly hour. He has told the police that he only did it to find out if Ally McCoist could see them.

I am trying not to laugh, but not knowing if the sergeant finds it funny, I stop myself, and the guy tells me that he will be providing Mr Gascoigne with a bed and some breakfast and he can be picked up any time after half past six the next morning.

I return to bed again, half-laughing but half-worried, knowing that this will get back to Walter and he is going to kill us. The following morning, I'm up early. I drive to the police station, and there is Gazza at the bottom of the steps, a blank stare on his face. I pull up, he opens the passenger door and, without looking at me, he sits down and puts his seat belt on, pauses and then says, 'Not one of my better ideas.'

To be sat with Paul Gascoigne in my car at 6.45 a.m., me doubled over with laughter, these are memories I will never forget, but when I think of my English pal, it isn't all madness. There is such a gentle side of his character too, and one story underlines that.

It also confirms that he was a wee bit of an eavesdropper, because once again it starts with me chatting to a teammate saying it is my son's birthday, and on hearing the news, Gazza asks what my son is after in the way of a present. I tell Gazza that he loves animals and we are wondering what pet to get him.

Later that early evening, I'm sat in the living-room and my missus comes in and says she thinks she has seen someone at the end of the drive, and I should go and have a look. I get there and I am greeted with the following. There is a beautiful fish tank and a goldfish in a bag, there is a bird cage and in it are two budgies, a green one and a blue one, and there is the most beautiful, ornate rabbit hutch with the most gorgeous white bunny sat contently in it. Next to them all are bags providing a load of food for each animal and on top of that is a card, with the words: 'Dear Alexander, have a great birthday, Gazza.'

That sums the man up. For all the mayhem, for all the crazy stories, and there are plenty, the guy has a heart of gold.

So, like the time I've spent with Gazza, my relationship with the auld enemy down south has had its crazy moments and its heartwarming moments. Like so many Scots, there are not many things that bring a wee smirk to the face quite like seeing that lot get beat, be it at football or tiddlywinks, and for the rest of my days, I'll be hoping that never changes.

But like all neighbours who don't always see eye-to-eye, the best thing to do is share a drink and raise a glass every now and then. I'm more than happy to do so, but when I do, believe me there will be one name I'll be toasting. Alexander Watson Hutton. G'aun yersel', big man.

Disclaimer: Ally McCoist appreciates that his playing record for Scotland vs England reads as follows: Played 4, Drew 1, Won 0, Lost 3, Goals Against 5, Goals For 0 twelve

NO PARTY!

M Y legs are weary, my mind is tired, and I'm finding it hard to understand authoritative instructions. No, I'm not in Scotland's midfield, I am a man who has travelled a fair few miles in less than a month. Now, after a quick visit home, I am at Edinburgh airport heading back to Germany for the latter stages of the Euro 2024 tournament.

The place is jam-packed with north-east English boys off to see the quarter-finals of the championships, plus loads of Scots who had got themselves tickets for the latter stages. It's a great atmosphere, with good patter flying about, but as I am standing there waiting to go through security, a bit late for my flight, the guy working there notices the gormless look on my face brought on by a month of planes, trains and German automobiles. He takes pity on me and rushes me to the front.

I put my bag through the scanner, I walk through, and there's a loud bleep. I look at him with the stare of a man who has never travelled before. He rolls his eyes. East-coast expletives roll quietly from his mouth.

'Have you got anything in your pockets?'

I empty my pockets, and I have car keys and about sixteen quid in loose coins. He's exasperated. He grabs my hand, points up to the very large sign in big red letters: EMPTY YOUR POCKETS AND PUT ITEMS IN THE TRAY.

'Do you see that sign? Can you read it? That's exactly what it fuckin' means.'

He sends me back, I put my keys and the cash in the tray, walk back through, and the beep goes off again.

'Have you got a belt on?'

I nod and he looks at me, shakes his head, and says, 'It'll take me fucking all day to check you. On you go!'

His colleague in security has seen it all, and she shouts, 'To be fair to him, it's his first flight in about twenty-four hours!'

She's not wrong. The month has been an exhilarating adventure in the clouds, on the road and on the tracks, and as battle weary as I now am, I wouldn't change a thing. To move around Germany and feel very much part of the summer's festival of football has been a privilege, one that has introduced me to so many new aspects of European football, most of them positive, whilst confirming how much our game brings people together.

But, of course, as a Scot desperate to see our lot progress, the wind has been taken from my sails (with hindsight perhaps on that first night in Munich) and along with tens of thousands of like-minded and well-travelled souls, the end against the Hungarians in Stuttgart feels like a punch in the stomach, mainly because the match itself is such a damp squib.

Hungary's goal, in what feels like the 186th minute, is one of those moments. Déjà vu? A lifetime of watching, hoping, playing and trying, and as the Hungarians break from our corner, that lifetime flashes before my eyes. Some say it is a goal that you can see coming a full minute before the ball hits the net. I disagree. It's a goal we could all see coming some fifty years ago, when a nation began to believe in its possible glory, only for us all to be hit on the break, those hopes shattered once again.

What hurt the most was that the game never got going. Not once were the players able to find the energy that the match and more importantly the occasion required. I am doing the game with Seb Hutchinson, and there are moments throughout the match when we are looking at each other in bemusement, because nothing is happening. Both teams have to win, both teams have to find something extra, but the game simply won't ignite, and it's infuriating.

The whistle goes and for one brief moment, there is silence from our otherwise vocal and magnificent supporters. A kind of collective sigh. A knowing and well-practised release of disappointment. I have empathy with the players, I know how much they would have wanted to do well, I know how much they wanted to be the group who finally made dreams come true and all that hope a glorious reality. I've been there. All you can do is applaud the people, give the media answers to their questions about wishing it had been different. Platitudes. That's all that is humanly possible to muster.

Before I put down my microphone, my gaze and thoughts turn to Stevie Clarke. I know Steve well, I played with him, he is a top man and a fantastic coach, and looking at him, I can only imagine how disappointed and alone he must be feeling. A whole nation, behind you and your team, is now questioning your tactics and methods. There is nothing wrong with that and Steve would agree. That's the game. That's management.

I for one sympathised with the manager. Certain things went against him in terms of decisions and injuries, but what cannot be denied is that the team were too defensive, or should that be too within themselves, to break out and show any creativity. It might have been the shock of the Germany defeat and its magnitude, but in the next two games that required a victory, there was not enough magic to dominate and create.

The team lacked width, wide-men willing and able to beat a defender, take him out and force overloads. Andy Robertson is some player, one of our greats, but he is a full-back, he can cause chaos with a great delivery, but we needed that player who can take people on.

Up front, Che Adams was the most willing runner. You could wring his shirt out with the sweat he created for the cause, but it was a thankless and futile exercise. I have been there too. I have been asked to be the lone striker, especially against teams with more of the ball, and whilst you will run and run, the ball doesn't stick and you are left chasing shadows.

I think the injury to Lyndon Dykes was key. Dykes up front would have been more suited to the style of play adopted. It might not have been pretty, but the big man's game is holding the ball up, winning the team territory as well as possession. Scotland needed to get up the pitch, allow players to join from midfield, or even win set pieces in and around the opponents' box.

I also wanted to see more of Lawrence Shankland up top. Especially when we needed goals. Even in his short cameos, I could see the kind of runs he wanted to make, the sort of space he was looking to exploit, and you can tell he's a goalscorer. There is a big difference between players who score goals, and goalscorers, and Shankland has the natural instinct that the team craved.

The major problem Steve Clarke had though was in midfield, the place on the park that looked to be his strongest when the competition began. In truth, none of John McGinn, Scott McTominay, Callum McGregor or Billy Gilmour got going to the level we all know they can.

These were all factors in the team's inability to ensure a vital victory, but they were also unlucky in places, especially late on in the Hungary game when they might have been given a penalty. On another night they would have, but once again, the inconsistency around penalty kicks had us all wondering what was what.

When Stuart Armstrong broke from midfield, I was imploring him to take the shot, but perhaps expecting the foul, he delayed and when the challenge came, the referee, an Argentine called Facundo Tello, kept his whistle dry. 'Just physical contact' was UEFA's official line, and one that had Scots tearing their hair out.

For commentators like me, my eye and my patriotism were compromised. My first and honest reaction was no penalty.

Maybe it was my striker's instinct, but I thought Armstrong took too long. When I watched it a few times, though, my mind changed; yes, he waits and waits, but that drew the foul and if it was 'just physical contact', it was also foul play.

Leaving the stadium, the first person I bumped into was Pat Nevin. We stopped to chat about the game and he told me quickly that, in his opinion, it was never a penalty. It is fine margins and, as usual, Scotland find themselves left in them.

You have to have sympathy with the manager, and after the game I could sense that Steve was biting his tongue about the penalty and the fact that the referee was South American. It did seem strange that UEFA couldn't find European officials to ref their games, but with the dust settled, Steve would be the first to admit that the referee's place of birth had nothing to do with the team's failings.

Having said that, I cannot ever see a time when a Scot referees a game between Argentine teams, and I chuckle at the thought of the great Hugh Dallas officiating the River Plate vs Boca Juniors fixture. To be honest, having been the man in the middle for several Old Firm derbies, the Buenos Aires derby might offer some light and welcome relief.

Unfortunately, the sometimes poor standard of refereeing and the dreaded VAR continue to be a topic of conversation, and I do feel that the refs are too often officiating with VAR in the back of their minds. Natural refereeing has gone. Decisions are being made in the knowledge that voices can come to their ears, instructions can be given to recheck screens, and we now have a game that is slightly lost.

Look at the handball decisions. We have to go back to the word 'intent'. I did the Germany vs Denmark Round of 16 fixture. Crystal Palace's Joachim Anderson has a goal ruled out for a tight offside, okay, fair enough, but then, seconds later he is penalised for a handball that can only be described as farcical.

The defender is defending and the ball grazes his thumbnail. How can that be a penalty and what is with this 'unnatural position' of the arm nonsense? Anyone who has played the game knows that being asked to keep the arm behind the back is the most unnatural position and asking players to do that is ridiculous.

There is also the penalty given to England in their semifinal against the Dutch. I was doing co-comms and couldn't believe that VAR were looking at the incident, let alone that they gave the spot kick. Kane kicks the defender! Sam Matterface is saying that he'd be very surprised if it was given, and then from the corner of my eye I see the ref being called to the little screen. 'I have good news for the English,' I say. 'I'd be very surprised if, having been asked to have a look, he doesn't.'

England go on to win the game, with Ollie Watkins' late strike, and I am sat with Sam and Lee Dixon. Sam is understandably going mad on commentary, and Lee is up punching the air. Unsure of what to do, I am as enthusiastic as any proud Scot can be, and offer a slow round of applause. As part of the striker's guild, I am more than impressed with Watkins' finish, and give my congratulations accordingly.

It is the next day that I am informed that some of my compatriots back home have taken my involvement in the commentary box and the fact that I did not stand up and boo England's winner as somehow being unpatriotic.

It's an eye-opener. The amount of hatred someone can get on social media platforms for the smallest thing. Actually a lot of it is very funny. One offended individual writes, 'ENGLAND CAN KEEP THE BOOT-LICKING BASTARD!' I can safely inform the gentleman who wrote these words, that having shown some English colleagues your comments, I am not wanted by them either!

However, I was wanted in the commentary box for the final and witnessed Spain's late winner, which I thought was a brilliantly worked goal, and one that guaranteed the competition was won by its best team. There is no bravado from me, no anti-England rhetoric comes from my mouth, just a quiet sense of wellbeing that the Spaniards got what they deserved.

It is interesting, from a Scottish point of view, to be around the English and pick up the negativity that goes with following their nation's football team. My take on it is, there remains a sense of superiority amongst some fans. A slight forgetfulness in the fact that this is tournament football and the likes of Denmark, Serbia and Slovenia are there for a reason, which is not merely to make up the numbers. Sure, some of the earlier games were not classics, but the job is to win the group and that job was done. As a Scot in the presence of many conversations, I can only wish for five points in a group stage that we have won.

On the matter of the so-called smaller nations, I do believe they are the summer's biggest success. The performances of these less fashionable sides were, for me, the standout, and none were better than Georgia. The Georgians finished some nine points behind Spain and Scotland in the qualifying stages and were only there because of a good Nations League campaign.

But they lit up the tournament. Their defeat to Turkey was possibly the best game in the group stages, and their defeat of Portugal was a game to make the heart soar. Their football is constantly front-foot (a compliment you cannot pay to the majority of teams, including the bigger nations), their attitude is constantly positive and their supporters are amongst the many raucous and colourful groups travelling across Germany.

Not that it is always easy to articulate their talent.

I am working on the Georgia vs Turkey game for ITV and for the first time, Darren Bent is on co-comms for talkSPORT. Benty is a great lad, and is asking for some advice, especially when it comes to coping with some of the Georgian and Turkish names.

I show Darren my many notes, and I tell him the best way is to do it phonetically, and he takes a closer look at my own handwritten notes and how I have written my own phonetic versions of the guys playing. He is running his eye over them all. Sandro Altunashvili. Darren is looking confused.

'Olt-un-ush-vili? Coisty, that's not phonetic.'

I take another look.

'It is actually, Benty,' I say. 'It's just that they are written phonetically in Glaswegian . . . and by the way, you don't want to see what I have written down for Giorgi Gocholeishvili!'

The whole summer working with great people like Darren Bent is as close as it comes to playing, and one of my favourite teammates on these occasions is Clive Tyldesley. Clive is like a big brother in the commentary box, a legend who has seen it all, covered the biggest of games and given us the best of lines to match the best occasions, and it is always a pleasure to work with him.

If I say something up there that he thinks is cretinous, which is quite often by the way, he will give me that side glance, that look that tells me he is tired of working with amateurs. We do plenty of games together, and it is always a pleasure to return to the hotel after a game and sample a bottle of wine with him whilst digesting the match we have just seen.

Plenty of people were disappointed that Clive finished commentating on the Euros after the Round of 16 game, and I understand why. He had a contract and that decision was nothing to do with me. Am I sad that he's leaving ITV? Yes, I am, but I know that we will work together soon, and I am also buoyed by the knowledge that football commentary in the UK is in great hands with a new generation consisting of the likes of Sam Matterface, Seb Hutchinson and Darren Fletcher.

But now it is time to say goodbye to Germany. I've loved every minute of it. Sure, some of the football wasn't the most attacking we've seen and classic football matches were in short supply, but that's all on the pitch. For me, the true success of a tournament is off the pitch, and seeing people from all four corners of the continent, mingling, laughing and singing, has offered memories that will last.

As ever, Scotland's success came in the shape of its people, not its football team. It's something we have got used to but nevertheless, it is a fact that we should all be very proud of. Before the last group game against Hungary in Stuttgart, the city was given a rendition of bagpipes that stopped the city centre. I have heard the instrument played on many occasions by individuals perhaps not in the right state to do so, but on this occasion the pipes were a perfect soundtrack to the fun that the Tartan Army brought to Germany's summer.

On the pitch, it wasn't to be. Once again, the people's hopes were dashed, but once the dust has settled and the hangovers cured, dreams will resurface and plans will be made. In two years, all being well, our nation will temporarily migrate across the Atlantic.

You never know, next time might be our time, and even if not, you know what they say . . .

'No Scotland, No Party!'

epilogue

THE HOPE WON'T KILL US

'WE'RE the only team in the world that does a lap of disgrace ...'

As someone who has experienced the pain of the referee's final whistle in the last game of a major tournament – and knows that sound as one that has always ushered in only frustration and regret – it is hard to hear Billy Connolly's classic joke without feeling the urge to wince.

The Big Yin might be the best at telling the joke, but he certainly won't be alone amongst long-suffering Scots with that seemingly never-ending sense of footballing déjà vu, or on his own in thinking that maybe laughter is all we, as a country, have left.

With our national team's exasperating knack of returning home from major tournaments before the postcards, perhaps that is something to be proud of. Can our ability to laugh at ourselves override any sporting difficulties we may show?

Rather than mulling over and over the endless technical reasons why Scotland never progress into the knockout stages of international competitions, should we just bask in the glory of making it there in the first place?

Let's do that for moment. Let's look at how this country of a little over five million people has forged a relationship with a global event that, every four years, attracts five billion pairs of eyes. The World Cup. Two hundred nations vying to be there, with every corner of the planet involved some-how from the off, and whilst FIFA is ever-expanding the size of the finals, there can be no denying that the Scots have made a considerable impact. If the saying is 'punching above your weight', Scotland have regularly donned their gloves, stood up on a stool and thrown some hefty shots at the big boys.

Scotland's initial dalliance with the World Cup came in 1950, when the winner and the runner-up of that year's British Home Championship were invited to take part in the tournament being held in Brazil. The men in suits though, with a wonderful example of puritanical self-flagellation, decided that Scotland would only travel if we won the championships.

Predictably, we came second to England and remained at home. Looking back, it was a peculiar decision, and even the knowledge that the English were beaten out there by the United States and came home early, didn't make it any less frustrating.

It was four years later that the Scots made their global entrance, but this time the Football Association decided that such a competition required only thirteen players (eighteen

FA officials and their wives travelled) and the heavy cotton shirts usually worn in Glasgow on a February afternoon.

Maybe it was the venue, Switzerland, that tricked them into thoughts of chilly Alpine pastures, and they neglected to discover that, unlike Scotland, the Swiss have warm summers. Instead, having lost their first game to Austria, the team were sent out in their heavy shirts for a match in the hot Basel sunshine against the holders, Uruguay, who were wearing lightweight shirts and looked far more at home. The South Americans ran out 7–0 winners, and Tommy Docherty, our right-half on the day, later admitted, 'We were knackered by the end of the anthems.'

Four years later, in Sweden, Scotland were once again there and fared marginally better by drawing one game, but then that was it. The 1960s stood out for the frustration of watching from afar as another minor nation won the thing, but then in the mid-1970s, it was us who travelled to Germany and then Argentina, the sole flag bearers for British football on the world stage.

And that set the tone. From 1974, Scotland went on to qualify for six out of seven World Cups, and within that spell, there was the garnish of two back-to-back European Championships. It was an astonishing period of success that I would argue, when it comes to the smaller nations, can only be matched in world football by the incredible achievements of Croatia; an even smaller nation than ours, but one that continues to produce a frankly ridiculous amount of world-class footballers.

Even today, Scotland are throwing those punches, vying to be seen on the football pitch as much as the fans who follow them are seen and loved off it. So there you have it, consistent and competitive, time and time again there, our fans making friends, the team trying (but failing) to make history. That's enough, isn't it? The real achievement is getting there, right . . . well, isn't it?

The thing is, as much as that might be factually correct, I absolutely hate that school of thought with a passion. I want no part of it. Of course, it's fantastic that we consistently make tournaments, but with all my soul, I detest comments like, 'Ach well, we're only wee,' or even worse comments (mainly from down south) like, 'Ahhh, Scotland, didn't they do well, just being there?'

When people celebrate the Scottish football team as 'competitors', I hear 'also-rans'. It may be irrational, especially coming from someone who played in several tournaments, and is even proud of how we performed in a couple of them, but who said this has to be rational? For me, if this nation is going to progress as a footballing presence, we have to reject that sense of perennial and inevitable disappointment.

The comedian Harry Enfield once did a sketch on his TV programme. Set up as a Pathé News film from post-war Britain, it had two English fans, with clipped BBC accents, politely celebrating another England success. One says, 'Spare a thought for those plucky losers.' They begin to clap. 'Bad luck, Scotland.' I mean we can laugh at ourselves, and frankly, thank heavens for that, but we have to use such sneering perceptions to drive us on to a successful future.

This is where I get the blue and white face paint on, mount my horse (will my bike do?) and rally the nation, underlining that with a can-do attitude, this great footballing land of ours can make strides from backwater to powerhouse. Why not?

For too long, the narrative has been about a distant yearning for success. A kind of unreal aspiration rather than concrete belief. Even in 1982, when the squad travelled to Spain with trophy-winning stars such as Kenny Dalglish, Graeme Souness, John Robertson and someone called Alan Brazil, they went with a World Cup song, not about impending glory, but childlike delusion. 'We Have a Dream', it was called. You'll remember it. 'We hope and pray' say the lyrics, but I say enough of hope, enough of prayers, let's back ourselves, take pride in what we have as a country already given the world, and take our new steely attitude into the tournaments of the future.

I mean look at the individuals we can continue to celebrate. The best Bond in Connery, the best comedian in Connolly, the best schoolboy impersonator in Janette Krankie! I've seen first-hand how Scots at the top of their field are appreciated by global audiences. In 1996, prior to the European Championships in England, Scotland were on our tour and in training camp in the United States. We were in Connecticut, and Craig Brown, the manager, said, 'Right, lads, we've tickets for Rod Stewart at Madison Square Gardens,' or as they like to say in the business, 'The Garden'.

We were all overjoyed. Browny reiterated that we would train first, and then when we were there, we were to have one, maybe two beers at best whilst we enjoyed Rod's dulcet tones. We got to the Garden, and of course, word got to Rod that the boys were in. As a passionate football man and avid Scotland fan, he got a load of us up there on stage with him, and if anyone has any footage of the moment, it is very clear by the way we are banging out 'Maggie May' that Browny's suggestion of one, or maybe two beers has been utterly and severely ignored.

But the point is, that's what Scotland can bring to the world, and that's why I think our football, like us willing entertainers that night, can shine on the biggest stage. Some say not, the doomsayers suggest that our youth are no longer bothered and the next generation has gone soft, even lamenting the demise of tenements and coal mines as places from which our many footballing greats emerged.

Yes, that's true, the world has changed, but I am not having it that Scottish youngsters are unwilling to be seen and compete again. I see the form in a country housing as few people as ours as being cyclical. We've had our golden generations, as they like to call them in England, and we have had some copper generations too, that is only normal, but do not tell me that golden nuggets will not rise from our game again.

I have managed at club level and I have assisted at international level, and I have seen the natural enthusiasm for the game in our country. I have seen the desire in our youngsters to play, to develop and to progress. Where they need help is at that initial stage, and it is noticeable that we need to create more small pitches where kids can go and play, be it coached and organised, or simply a kick-about with pals.

I've seen close up how reticent councils are to help facilitate such areas, but without them, those negative comments that the youth of today are only interested in being on their phones, or inside on their laptops, will become a worrying truth.

Our clubs can do more, too. The academies around the country have had some success, and clubs such as Dundee United and Hamilton Academical should be applauded for their efforts to promote youth and give homegrown players a real crack at the professional game.

The Scottish FA itself commissioned a report in the summer of 2024 looking at the issues, the incentives to change things, and the trends to follow that will ensure that the talent in this country – and there is still an abundance of it – gets a real chance to flourish.

A major issue that football has in Scotland, like most leagues, is the short-termism approach to management. With the constant fear of losing their jobs in what is strongly a results business, head coaches and managers are reluctant to give the necessary game time to players in the 16–18 age bracket.

There is a talent pool. It might be shallower than it once was, but when you see youngsters such as Ben Doak going to Liverpool from Celtic and Rory Wilson going to Aston Villa from Rangers, there is proof of life within it.

It won't be easy, but when has it ever been, and let's not contrast any future footballers we produce against names from the past. Any country in the world, I don't care who they are – Spain, Germany, Brazil or Argentina – would do well to produce talent on a par with names such as Law, Dalglish and Souness. With some work, some dedication and collective cooperation, Scotland can continue to provide the national team with talent and yes, it can make it to major tournaments with far more ambition than merely making up the numbers.

It's a thought that takes me right back to May 1978, stood amongst 30,000 other hearty souls, with smiles across our faces, tartan scarves around our necks and wrists. Seeing off the boys on their travels across the Atlantic, with merriment and joy. That sense of belief, a collective, tangible and real faith that we could seriously compete with the world's best. Of course it was misplaced, but give me that initial belief over dismal assumption any day of the week.

As I have said, my life in football has taken me everywhere, put me amongst the best people anyone could meet, and looking back on it, all I can do is smile and laugh. But there also comes a time to look forward and when it comes to the national team, I'll be doing so with all the brash enthusiasm that I did back then, aged fifteen.

We are, after all, on the march . . .

ACKNOWLEDGEMENTS

I love that football keeps me busy and what with a lot of media work, some have wondered if there is in fact more than one of me. Luckily for everyone, I can report that there is not and like everything I have ever done, it's all about teamwork. Putting this book together has been no different.

I want to thank Huw Armstrong and all his team at Hodder. Niamh Anderson, Charlea Charlton, Lizzie Dorney-Kingdom, Rebecca Mundy and Inayah Sheikh Thomas, thank you for your hard work. I hope you agree that it's been worth it. Thank you to Tony Clarke and Paula McGuckin at Soccer Speaker for all their help; and to Nick Walters at David Luxton Associates, for convincing me to take the plunge. I want to thank Leo Moynihan, who helped get my many thoughts and memories down on paper, and for laughing at (most of) my jokes.

Last but very far from least, I want to thank my wife, Vivien, for everything she does.

PICTURE CREDITS